T0339819

# May I have this Dance

### CONNIE MANSE NGCABA

face2face

Published in 2014 by Face2Face
an imprint of Cover2Cover Books (Pty) Ltd
www.cover2cover.co.za

©2014 Connie Manse Ngcaba

ISBN: 978-0-9922017-9-1

Editing: Clarity Editorial www.clarityeditorial.co.za
Proofreading: Martin Rollo
Cover & book design: Design for development
Inside cover photograph: Thys Dullaart
All other photographs courtesy of the author
Typesetting: Design for development www.d4d.co.za
Printed and bound in South Africa by Paarl Media, Cape Town.

# May I have this dance

*The story of my life*

Connie Manse Ngcaba

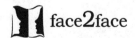 face2face

# CONTENTS

# NGCABA FAMILY TREE

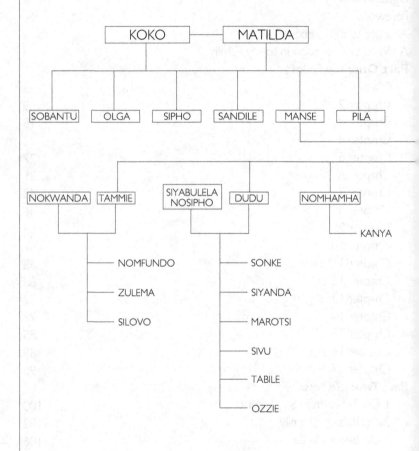

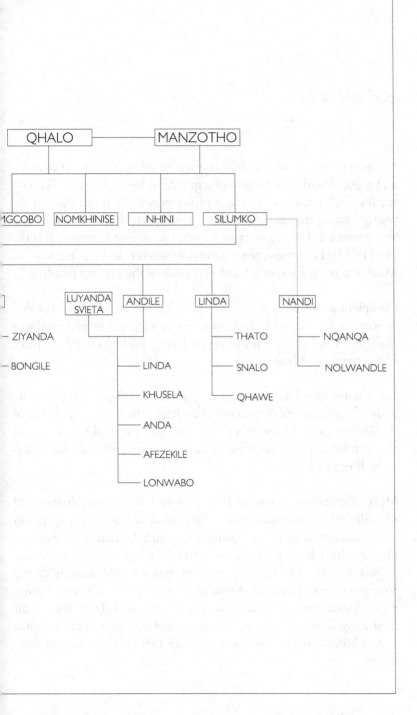

QHALO — MANZOTHO

MGCOBO — NOMKHINISE — NHINI — SILUMKO

LUYANDA SVIETA — ANDILE — LINDA — NANDI

ZIYANDA

BONGILE

THATO — NQANQA

SNALO — NOLWANDLE

QHAWE

LINDA

KHUSELA

ANDA

AFEZEKILE

LONWABO

# FOREWORD

I finished writing this book at the age of 84. I am a mother of six and a grandmother to twenty-two grandchildren. This story is about my life during the various stages of my growth. It is the story of the young Manse, the girl who had to grow up quickly, then fell in love and got married. It is a story of Mama, the wife and mother. It is the story of MaHlongwane, the community worker, and it is the story of Makhulu, the grandmother and matriarch of the Ngcaba family.

Completing this book was a very proud moment for me. I decided to write it for the perfectly human reason of pride in overcoming a challenge. I feel a deep sense of joy for having pushed myself to a place I have never been before.

I also wrote this book to make a small contribution to the existing body of written work that portrays the determination and resilience of the African spirit. I hope that those who read it will take what lessons they can from it, and use these in their own lives to build a life that is rewarding and fulfilling.

My desire has always been that I should live a meaningful and rewarding life, pursuing knowledge, creativity and self-expression while contributing to my community and humanity in general. This is why I have always been active in programmes for change, at first through my work as a nurse and my affiliation with the Young Women's Christian Association, and in recent years through my childcare centre. Children are the future and helping them with their early learning and development has been my career of choice as Makhulu. I had to respond to the call that children were making to me.

The political transformation in 1994 brought with it tremendous shifts in the lives of our people. It brought freedom and an enabling political, social and economic environment. As a mother who took part in the fight for political change and had her own life – and those of her family members – severely affected, I knew I had to write this book as a way to examine our current society in the hopes that we can learn to be resilient, embrace the change and yet constantly affirm ourselves as a people.

The family is a sacred institution. It is an essential building block for a great nation. If there is no cohesion, if we lack the glue that holds family members together, it will be difficult to build strong families and a strong nation. We should do all we can to preserve it.

This book is also a gift to my grandchildren. I hope they will page through this book, look at the photographs and shriek with laughter at how old-fashioned everything seems. I also hope they will read my story and get a better perspective of how things used to be, and the role the mother plays in African society. If you cannot appreciate where you came from, you will not know how to envision your future.

My life has afforded me experiences that I think are similar to the life of a tree. If you can imagine a tall oak tree, with very deep roots, a powerful trunk and strong, yet flexible branches that produce colourful, appealing leaves, then you get a picture of who I am today. It is my hope that this book will encourage women to want to become like an oak tree as they take their partners' hands in building their families and, in so doing, build a powerful nation.

# A LETTER TO MY HUSBAND

*Dear Bro Sol*

*Two years ago, when l was drafting this book, I gave it to you to read. In it was another letter to you, in which I acknowledged that we would soon, inevitably, be reaching the end of our journey together. Little did l know that my prediction would come true before the book would go to print.*

*On 8 January 2013, in a hospital at a quarter to twelve, the angel of death took your soul from your body, leaving me with your motionless remains. I will never forget that moment as long as I continue my human journey alone.*

*As in a dream, almost all our children surrounded us, saying a farewell prayer. Emotionally l did not want to let go, but l knew l had to respect the process of death. I had to give you over to the cold earth, where you were buried, deep down, in a wooden coffin.*

*My grief can never be measured. I shall always treasure the memories of our union of sixty years. Thank you, dear, for helping me reach this age, for supporting all my efforts and trusting me with what you had for all these years. You never gave me a moment of regret, a moment of doubt or even a moment of mistrust. I am grateful to God for giving me the opportunity to be a wife to a man who honoured his word to the end.*

*Rest in peace, my love*

*Manse*

# A WORD OF APPRECIATION TO MY FAMILY

*Parents are the essential building blocks in the creation of any individual. On behalf of Sol and myself, I am honoured to have this opportunity to thank our family for the support and the comfort they have offered us, especially during our retirement.*

*A powerful and a prosperous family is a family whose children respect the investment of their parents in their lives. Your actions and how you conduct yourselves witnesses the balanced guidance you received when you were brought up. Your achievements have filled our hearts with joy. The world out there is watching how you conduct yourselves as respected parents and loyal citizens of our country. The type of the nation we all wish for depends on the excellence you strive to achieve.*

*The solid, wise foundation you acquired from your father can take you to the sky if you are serious enough never to abandon your family values.*

*My promise to you all is that, if health permits, one day you will witness your mother put her signature at the bottom of the first copy of her book. Be thankful to be adults who still say "mama" – at your age, a rare opportunity.*

*Your departed father and I appreciate your presence in our world, your attitude towards our family values and your enthusiasm about life in general. We love you dearly, and fortunately you do not doubt that.*

*Love*

*Mama*

# PART I THE FOUR M'S

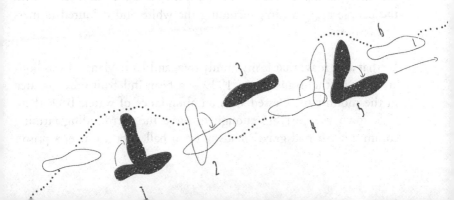

I

We all come from a family. That is the one thing we have in common. A family is a powerful force, capable of writing and changing the destiny of every person in it. Just as a child being born transforms a man and a woman into a father and a mother, so parents shape their children's futures by teaching them certain values and showing them how to be in this world. The direction in which a family grows – either towards success or despair – is determined by the interaction between generations past and those yet to come.

The family tree at the beginning of this book shows only a small branch of my ancestry. It doesn't show that my grandfather on my father's side was married twice and fathered six children. It does not tell the story of how he stood up to tribal law and he decided to raise his sister's illegitimate child (fathered by a white man) as his firstborn rather than allow the child to grow up in the home of his mother's parents.

That family tree also doesn't tell how my ancestors followed the missionaries from Swaziland down to what is now the Eastern Cape, settling at Khobodi near Butterworth. Neither does it show my grandfather's ties to the land. Mankayi Silwana was an avid farmer, deeply involved with the land. He learnt much of what he knew from the missionaries. The rest stemmed from his ability to interact with the people around him, including the white and coloured farmers and traders.

Be that as it may: that is my family tree, and I am Manse. I was born at Cala, in the Transkei, in 1929 – a beautiful fruit-growing area in the mountains, blessed with an abundance of water. Back then, Cala town was just big enough to serve the surrounding farming community. It had gravel roads, a town hall, a post office, a prison and some white-owned shops, many belonging to the farmers in the area.

My parents named me Manse, which means joy; for joy is what they felt at the birth of the youngest girl in my grandmother's house. Those were the days of extended families, where the grandfather remained the head of the large extended family.

My second name is Constance, after a local white shop owner who was a hardworking and very generous soul. Even though the apartheid system was a dark cloud in the country's future, segregation and oppression were already the norm. Yet even at that time there were many white people who broke the mould and embraced African people with respect and humanity.

The Constance after whom I was named would gladly allow the members of the community to purchase much-needed foodstuffs on account. She was rewarded with customers who would be faithful and pay when money became available. That woman showed the kind of trust that my husband would show in me, so many years later. His trust empowered me to strive to live up to his expectations and be the best person I could be. He trusted me with everything and I was determined never to disappoint him. I am glad I was named Constance after that very kind and generous woman.

I was the second daughter born to my parents. My older sister, Olga Nomtshato, was born in November 1917. She was eleven years old when I was born. I also had three older brothers – Sobantu, Sipho and Sandile, whom we called Sandie.

Sandie left our home to live with Mama's sister, Elizabeth Ngcebetsha, when I was eight and he was twelve. Mamkhulu, or "older mother", as we called my aunt because she was ten years older than Mama, had trained as a teacher but never worked as one because she got married at an early age. Her husband had passed away, leaving her with a big home and over twenty head of cattle – not to mention sheep, goats, pigs and fowl of every feather – to look after. Sandie went to Mamkhulu's to help her look after these animals because all her children were grown up and married. I remember him being very excited about gaining his independence in this way. It was also an opportunity for him, because with two older brothers it wasn't likely that he would be given much authority at home any time soon.

My younger brother, Pila, was born when I was three and a half. Of all my siblings, I was always closest to Olga, my sister, and Pila, my younger brother. Even when he was born, there was always a spark of light in Pila's eyes. He was a survivor and he had the personal strength to work himself up in life and become successful. He ended up being a well-respected manager at a company called Cobra Springs. He did very well there, built himself and his family a beautiful home and retired gracefully after having served the company for thirty-five years. Imagine that. Thirty-five years! But I get ahead of myself.

Until I was nine years old, my childhood was complete. My father farmed the smallholding his father had given him. He farmed sorghum and beans, and pumpkins of such a high standard that the shops in the town eagerly bought them. My neighbours were my family, my father's three brothers and their families, who had each also inherited a smallholding, their share of the family farm that had been divided between my grandfather's sons. Our big garden was fenced. There were kraals for the livestock and two rondavels with a four-roomed flat: one room for my parents to sleep in, one for my brothers to sleep in, one for cooking and one for prayers and eating. While I was still small, this last big room was rearranged every evening to make sleeping place for Olga and me and the baby, Pila. There was also a sort of storeroom for uncooked food. When I was a little older, Mama arranged for one of the rondavels to be demolished and another big one to be built in the modern way, with modern furniture inside.

Mama gardened and took care of the house and the children. She always knitted us warm jerseys to keep the Cala cold at bay. We went to school and thrived under our parents' love and protection. As a family, we had enough to meet our needs and share with those less fortunate than us. I had the benefit of being much loved by my older siblings. Olga is now ninety-six years old but she still remembers how my two older brothers, Sobantu and Sipho, would fight among themselves to be the one to help me when I cried after a runaway ball. She herself would make dolls for me out of mielie cobs and sew dresses for them. Mama would be glad to see her older children look after the younger ones in this way.

This nurturing family environment instilled in me a sense of wholeness, well-being and self-assurance. Never did I feel the uncertainty of seeing my father leave to go work in the towns and the mines. Never did I have to watch Mama struggle with the isolation and helplessness I have seen so often in women when their husbands are away, turning to secret lovers or drinking. It never so much as occurred to us children that we might want to rebel against our parents and drop out of school.

My school career began in 1935 at Manzimdaka Lower Primary School, about an hour's walk from our home in Cala. I was six years old. We had to cross a river in order to get to school. My two brothers, Sobantu and Sipho, used to help me cross. Sobantu, our eldest brother, would go ahead of us, carefully pointing out stones that he instructed us to step on. I now realise that he was only one of many people who has helped show me the path in my life.

Manzimdaka Lower Primary went up to Standard Two and was housed in a Presbyterian church. The higher primary school was in an Anglican church, some way away. When I started, we sat on the floor and wrote with our slates on our laps. From Standard One we sat on benches, carefully copying whatever Miss Figlan wrote on her portable blackboard. Miss Pilly Figlan was a tall, middle-aged woman and our only teacher, one of the many Xhosa people in our area who had an English name. She taught all sixty of us, from Sub A to Standard Two.

After school we would walk home, chatting happily together with our friends. We played touch and ran races against each other – the three-legged race was a firm favourite. Sometimes we would use grass to make a ball or skipping rope. We fought and made up and fought again. The animosity never lasted long.

My best friends in primary school were Muriel Mtyeku and Baza Dube. Muriel's father was a court interpreter and her mother made clothes. Baza's father was a school principal somewhere far away.

He rode a horse to school. Theirs was one of the best houses in Manzimdaka. It was made of brick and cement and had a couple of big rooms inside. Outside there was a big water tank. Although Baza's family did not have a farm, there were many chickens in their yard and ducks that swam in a small pond that was perpetually filthy.

One day, when I was about nine, the three of us were playing at the back with a big, homemade ball. One of us lost control of the ball and it rolled right into that grimy duck pond. We all rushed in to fetch it, but the pond floor was slippery and muddy. We could hardly stand, never mind climb out. Petrified, we called for help. I was beginning to worry that no one would hear us, when finally some boys came past and helped us out. Baza's mother cleaned us up and warned us to stay away from the pond. All I wanted to do was go home and tell Mama about this terrible thing that had happened.

The time just after school was always very lively in my house. When we got home we would jostle to tell our mother our stories for the day, pushing each other away from her lap in excitement. "Wait, wait!" we would cry. "I want to tell her this! I want to tell her that!"

Our mother would sit quietly on her chair, a deep, knowing smile on her lips, looking at us through the light of love shining in her eyes and then say, "All right, all right. Nomtshato, you are the eldest. You begin." The decision made, I would dutifully bide my time and wait to tell my story after my older brothers.

Being the second youngest meant that certain things were expected of me and I, in turn, could expect certain things. When I was growing up, a child's position in the family had particular significance. Respect for age and position was deeply entrenched in our society. The birth position of the first child lent to that child a subtle aura of filial respect from – and responsibility for – the rest of the siblings. So it is that the firstborn daughter is referred to as uMafungwashe. Boys, especially when they grew older, could often be heard saying, "Ndifunga ngo Dadewethu uMafungwashe. I swear by my firstborn sister's name."

I was only seven years old when we got the news that Olga had been accepted to train as a teacher at Clarkesbury Training School in Engcobo. She excelled and was appointed head girl. My parents were so proud that, when she came home for the holidays, a special celebration was prepared. We were all treated to a special meal of the choicest food – chicken, mutton, pudding and ginger beer. Remember, there were no restaurants in those days. All events and celebrations took place at home. This was how the bond of family solidarity was forged.

The one thing I remember very well about Cala was the cold. The mornings were freezing. Mama often said she wished the cold only lasted one day because the children would soon develop stubborn colds and flu. At school, Miss Figlan was very kind. When she saw I was shivering, she would keep all the doors and windows closed, even though the classroom got very stuffy.

At home, we made sure we had enough firewood, dried cow dung and paraffin to chase the cold away. We used a paraffin stove, known as Beatrice, to make tea. Like most people, we used an imbawula for cooking and baking. An imbawula is a homemade stove made out of half an oil drum or even an old metal bucket cut open at the bottom to allow you to feed wood into it. It was open at the top and the metal was pierced with holes all the way up it to draw in air and encourage the flame. The imbawula was lit outside and then taken inside for cooking once the smoke had died down. A pot would be rested on a strong piece of net placed over the flame for cooking. We children would huddle around the imbawula during the winter, getting as close to it as we could without burning ourselves.

My family members cared deeply for each other, looking out for each other, trusting each other. My grandparents had been influenced by the missionaries, and we their children and grandchildren lived a life tailored on the Christian and social principles they taught. Prayer was an important element of life.

I am firmly convinced, even now that I am a grandmother myself, that those who sincerely apply Biblical principles to their lives live to be successful, not only spiritually but also materially. The Bible talks about one generation living in such a way that it provides the stepping stones for the next. In South Africa today we talk about building generational wealth. We can only do so if we first build a strong spiritual and moral base for our families. Such is the foundation of joy, peace, happiness and success.

My parents were loving people. My father doted on Mama; she was his point of reference in all matters. "Hayi ke Mama, ubona njani wena Makasana? How do you see this matter? What is your opinion?" He was not after her unquestioning approval. He respected her as his partner and wanted confirmation that they were together in their responsibility of building a good family life for us.

I will never forget this one thing my father used to do. When he had saddled his horse before riding off to town, he would call, "Ntomb'am, uTata uyahamba ngoku. My daughter, your father is now leaving. Come, let me give you a ride on the horse." Those words were like music to my ears. I would come running towards him and he would gather me up onto the horse, sit me in front of him, crack his whip and give me a few turns.

I loved this ritual. I would snuggle up close so that I wouldn't fall off. Even today, when I close my eyes and recall those tender moments, I can actually feel my head against his strong chest. I can smell again the Palmolive soap on his skin. So close was I to my Dad. To add joy on top of joy, he would without fail bring us sweets or, especially at the end of the month, a delicious fruity cake.

# 2

---

Nineteen thirty-nine marked the end of the serenity that flowed through my early years like a deep, calm river. The dramatic change came one day in January. Life has taught me that if there is anything constant, it is change.

I remember this fateful morning as clearly as if it happened yesterday. Enoch, my father's brother, saddled up two horses. My father walked slowly, his one hand on his hip, out the door towards his horse. From the doorway where I stood, I saw him gently and lovingly brush his horse's neck. I could see his hands. They seemed incredibly thin to me. The beard on his face was thick and matted. He had probably not shaved for some days.

Just before he slowly and painfully mounted his horse, he called out, "Manse." I walked quickly towards him. This time, he did not pick me up. He did not say a word. Instead, he kissed my forehead. Then he rode the horse towards Mama, who was standing a few metres away. He lowered himself slightly and hugged her.

Then the two riders trotted off, slower than usual. I was young. I saw but I did not comprehend. My mind could not form the questions, why or what. There was an eerie silence as we stood and watched my father and uncle disappear over the hill. Everybody stood motionless. Everybody was quiet. It was like the quiet when a cat is preparing to pounce on a rat. The quietness of death preparing to pounce on us.

That evening, Uncle Enoch came home with both horses. He told us that my father had been admitted to hospital. Ten days later, there was another change. Our normally peaceful home turned into a stage play. The house was thick with people singing church songs, all of them looking sad. The atmosphere was heavy. Mama looked worried, drained. I wondered why her sisters were hovering around her, covering her with a blanket and fussing about her so much. It was all so puzzling. I couldn't understand why there was so much whispering going on among the adults.

Then someone told Olga that our father had died two days before and that the people were here to attend his funeral. Although I had an intellectual understanding of what it was, I had never before experienced death and regarded it as something to be experienced by other people. So, instead of crying and feeling sad, I felt anger towards whoever was responsible. I told myself there was no way my beloved father could be dead. He was not a cow or a horse in the road. He was my father and could never be dead.

I looked up at the sky and, speaking to God himself, said, "Yimistake. It's a mistake. My father is coming back." I knew in my heart of hearts that the mistake would soon be rectified. My father would never leave me.

The days ran into weeks, the weeks into months. I had to come to terms with the reality that the mistake would never be corrected. I had to accept, with a lump in my throat, that there was no mistake. All there was, was the reality that our lives had changed forever. With my father dead, we would never again be together as the family I had known. The sudden and clear loss of my father was followed by a slow and subtle unravelling of the fabric of the life I once knew.

Our firstborn brother, Sobantu, was twenty-two when our father died. In those days the initiation was at twenty-one years, so when our father died he was a krwala, a new man. As a new man, he was expected to wear the clothes of a new man – clothes that we, his family, were supposed to provide but didn't because my father had just died. Sobantu was now expected to find work to support his mother and five siblings; he had the responsibilities of manhood but not the fancy new clothes.

Sobantu was anxious to wear proper manhood clothes, so he decided to sell some sheep to buy himself these clothes. Unfortunately, our uncles expected him to discuss his intentions with them first. They wanted him to explain to them when and how he would be seeking employment. They were angry, and in their anger ordered Sobantu to find work at the mines.

Sobantu was reluctant. It was common knowledge that miners could neither read nor write, and he was a Standard Six graduate. He knew he could do better. There were rumours that young men of any colour could join the army, as long as they were over eighteen. Sobantu grabbed the opportunity, joining the army at the end of that painful year. The Second World War was burning through North Africa and Europe at the time, and the recruitment system was strong. We were told that the government was looking for African manpower in North Africa, not to fight on the front but to drive trucks, carry stretchers and make boots – to provide the labour to do the tasks that kept the war machine turning over.

These jobs were still dangerous. Many African soldiers, my cousin Erasmus among them, died in North Africa. Some of these were buried in communal graves with dead white soldiers – that is, until the South African army headquarters found out about this and ordered that black and white casualties be buried separately. African soldiers received smaller allowances than white or coloured counterparts, and an African soldier was also only given an award if he was a stretcher-bearer, because they worked under very difficult conditions, tending to the wounded and transporting food right to the front line. Such was the thinking at the time.

Few African soldiers were given jobs when the war was over. Sobantu was one of the lucky ones – he was placed as a prison warder, driving the trucks that transported prisoners. He went on to get married and had three children, two sons and a daughter.

When my father was alive, the family made a living from farming, selling fruit and other produce. When he died, my older brother went off to war. Without my father and her eldest son, Mama struggled to work the farm. After six months of toiling through her grief, she admitted defeat and decided to seek work in Johannesburg, where her younger sister, Violet, was already working as a domestic.

What was going to become of us, now that our mother was going to work in Johannesburg? There was no way we could go with her. As a live-in domestic worker, she would have been given one small room to live in. There wouldn't have been space for us. Even if there was space, we would not have been able to go to school as there were only white schools in the suburbs. The townships were very far away.

Staying at Cala was also not an option. By now Olga was studying to be a teacher. My oldest brother was working in the mines and would soon be going off to war. Sipho was seventeen, old enough to remain at Cala under the watchful eye of my uncles and with the help of the homeless old woman who lived in an old storeroom. But my mother didn't want to leave me and my younger brother, Pila, with Sipho and this old lady. We had to find another place to call home.

It was eventually decided that we would join Sandie and the village orphans living with Mamkhulu in Zazulwana, near Butterworth. Two of Mamkhulu's adult children were working away from home and one of her sons had joined the army and was stationed in Egypt, where he eventually died. Mamkhulu had the space for more children and the need for extra hands to help maintain and protect her property. After Sandie joined her, she was inspired to open her house to needy children from the village. She had enough food to offer them and at the same time she needed them around her house. It was an arrangement that benefited everyone.

Eventually the day came when we were to travel to Zazulwana. We woke before dawn, the winter grass icy with frost. As we walked along the footpath down the hill, our mother held Pila with one hand and carried an old suitcase with our clothing in the other. I had to hold on tightly to her skirt as I walked, skipping every now and then to keep up. She walked briskly, worried that we would miss the only bus for the day from Cala to Butterworth. Though it was still dark I felt safe with her close to me. She kept talking to us, saying nice words to keep our hopes up, to help us make the best out of this situation.

We had not waited long when the rickety old bus arrived. The travellers were mostly miners going back to work. They were noisy, talking and shouting and laughing among themselves. We were quiet, more anxious than unhappy. It took the bus six hours to take us from Cala to Butterworth train station, stopping to drop off and pick up passengers many times during the 125-kilometre trip. When we got to the station, it took us another two hours to walk the six kilometres to Mamkhulu's house, Mama weighed down with our suitcase. It was only when we got there that our mother finally relaxed. At the gate of Mamkhulu's house a big dog welcomed us, wagging its tail and sniffing at Mama's hand. Perhaps it recognised us from our earlier Christmas visits.

Then Mamkhulu appeared, a smile on her face. "Molweni, bantakwethu," she said, hugging her sister and shaking our hands. Tears rolled down both women's cheeks. We went into the house and drank amasi. Mamkhulu then gathered everyone together for a welcome prayer and introduced everyone there. There were four women, most of them Mamkhulu's relatives, three boys and five girls. My heart smiled to see my brother Sandile among them. Young as I was, I could feel the warmth that permeated this big family.

Everyone seemed interested to meet Sandie's brother and sister, and Sandie himself was very excited to see us. "How long are you visiting?" he asked Mama after the prayer. "Don't go home too soon". Mama took him aside and spoke to him. I saw him nod. She told us later that he was committed to taking care of his siblings.

Everybody asked about our journey. After a delicious meal of mutton, vegetables and dumplings we went to bed, tired but happy. Early the following morning, after the morning prayers, Mama told the household that Pila and I were going to stay with them while she went to look for work in Johannesburg. In the bus on the way to Butterworth, the miners had been talking about how difficult their lives were in the mines. Mama had taken the opportunity to explain to us, and to me in particular, that that was why she was going to Johannesburg to work – so that she could pay for my education. I thought I understood at the time, but when she explained to everyone at Mamkhulu's that we would be staying behind, I felt rejected and unloved. I hid my feelings and promised her that I would look after Pila, but when she left a few days later I could not hold my tears. I found a private place, so that I would not be seen, and cried. It was the first time in my life that I would be apart from her. And then she was gone. I had no choice but to embark on the difficult journey to independence.

Before she left, Mama told me it was up to me to choose to make the best of my new life, and that doing so would help me emerge the best that I could be. I listened. I understood. I agreed. I knew that actions speak louder than words and was determined to be brave and reassure Mama that I did not feel as though she was abandoning me. I wanted her to leave knowing that I was managing my emotions, managing the change.

# 3

When Pila and I arrived, there were three boys and five girls in Mamkhulu's house. Of the boys there was Sandie, now aged thirteen; Mpondo, Mamkhulu's grandson, whose parents worked in Springs in the Transvaal; and Papase, who was nine. Papase had run away from his aunt who lived in the area.

The girls were mostly older. There was Nomzi, whose mother was working in East London, and Nogusha, whose father was a distant relative from Tsomo and had brought her to Mamkhulu's while he looked for work. Nogusha's mother drank and moved around a lot. Both Nomzi and Nogusha were fifteen.

There were also Nodosini, thirteen, and Tandiwe, eleven. Nodosini's mother was also a distant relative, and sick. Her father was away at work somewhere. Tandiwe's father was a former neighbour who now worked in the mines. He had left Tandiwe with her stepmother, who treated her cruelly. There was also Sitham who was Mamkhulu's granddaughter, Mpondo's sister. She was aged nine, just like me.

A few months after we arrived, our cousin, little Sidumo, joined us. His mother was Violet, my mother's younger sister who was already working in Johannesburg. Sidumo used to live with his grandmother on his father's side, but she died, so he came to Mamkhulu's.

So there we were: eleven children from different families all living together, making a home. It is no wonder that Mamkhulu was as strict as she was loving. She was like a boarding mistress who gave instructions that had to be followed to the letter by all. We soon learnt the routine and found ourselves saying "Yes, Mamkhulu", "Yes, Mamkhulu" as quickly and sharply as the others. Mamkhulu's farm had a three-bedroomed house, a two-roomed flat and three extra rondavels.

I shared a small room in the main house with Nomzi, Nogusha, Nodosini and Tandiwe. We all slept on floor mattresses. Mamkhulu slept in one of the bedrooms with her grandchildren, Sitham and Mpondo. The smart, well-furnished bigger bedroom was for Latiwe and her baby. Latiwe was Mamkhulu's daughter-in-law by her only living son, Erasmus, who was at the time a government worker at Stutterheim. This is the same Erasmus who later joined the army and died in Egypt during the Second World War. By that time Erasmus and Latiwe had four children together. Their second child was born in 1941 and their twins in 1943.

The boys slept on mattresses in the big rondavel. The smaller rondavel was for Mabhengu, Latiwe's cleaner and the nanny for her baby. Latiwe herself was a teacher at the local school, Zazulwana Primary. The flat housed Nogate, Mamkhulu's eldest daughter-in-law. Mamkhulu's son had died, leaving Nogate with three children, who stayed with Nogate's mother. Nogate was a dressmaker.

The children were organised into working groups according to their age and gender and assigned chores. Remember, in those days there was no inside plumbing, electricity or appliances to make things easier – everything had to be done by hand, and on a farm the size of Mamkhulu's there was a lot to be done.

I was put into the smaller children's group. Our duties were to wash dishes, make tea, collect and pack away eggs, clean the chicken coop, and wash and hang dishcloths. We also fetched water for washing ourselves from the nearby dam. This water wasn't suitable for cooking or drinking because the cows also drank from it, so it wasn't completely clean. Occasionally, if Mabhengu was busy, we would also be asked to look after Latiwe's baby.

On a normal school day, the older girls' group was responsible for fetching clean water from the nearby stream in the mornings and filling up the mortar with exactly the right amount of maize to be pounded into samp. In the afternoons, they collected kindling and dried cow dung to start an open fire in the kitchen for cooking samp and beans for dinner in Mamkhulu's large three-legged black pot. After serving the meal, they cleaned everything up again, ready for the next day's work.

During weekends, there were extra jobs to be done like collecting firewood and washing clothes in the river. We always looked forward to washing clothes, especially in summer, as we got a chance to swim while waiting for the clothes to dry on the grass because they would be too heavy to carry wet. At the river we met with other girls from the neighbourhood who had also come to do their washing. Many lasting friendships were formed over this weekly chore.

The boys were given the more physically challenging tasks of herding, feeding and milking the cattle. Some of the milk was used for tea and porridge. There were no refrigerators to keep the milk fresh in those days, so the leftover milk was poured into huge calabashes to thicken up and become delicious sour milk, which we ate with stiff, crumbly mielie-meal porridge, umphokoqho.

The boys were also responsible for ensuring that the sheep – of which Mamkhulu owned more than a hundred – were taken out to grazing lands and communal dipping grounds and safely returned to their pens at night. These sheep were sheared twice a year and the wool sold as a source of income. When the boys were at school Mamkhulu secured the services of a local herdboy.

At weekends, the boys used an ox cart to drag the water tank from the yard to the river to fill it up and chopped big branches off trees, collecting them with the same ox cart and stacking them away for rainy days or winter. Weekends were also a time of harvest, when a mixed group of boys and girls would collect fresh garden produce, which Mamkhulu insisted should be cooked and eaten while still very fresh. Other groceries were bought from town one Saturday a month. The opportunity to go along was given to those who could ride a horse.

Mamkhulu's regime of chores and obedience, while almost military, created a spirit of togetherness, healthy competition and determination in me. However, some of the other children reacted with outright anger. Many felt they were being exploited because they were orphans. There were murmurings of deep-seated rebellion, although the perpetrators never dared to erupt openly. I found it interesting that the more disadvantaged the child's background, the more that child responded with aggression, judgement and a sense of defeat.

This is not to say I felt no fears or insecurity. My parents had been taken from me and my life turned upside down. I remember the day that I stepped on a loose stone and twisted my ankle on my way back from helping the boys dip the cows. It was very sore and I cried bitterly. But I knew I was crying from the fact that I was missing Mama as much as the pain.

Fortunately, Olga was at Mamkhulu's for the school holidays. She came up to me, knelt down in front of me and gently hugged me to her chest. "Manse, just try to be strong. Mama will be back at Christmas." Not for the first time, I realised the benefit of having a sister much older than me. Olga was always there for us younger ones, teaching us and protecting us. Only she would have heard that voice of intuition inside her heart; that it was the pain of missing Mama that was making me cry so much!

Olga was my rock in those early days at Mamkhulu's. She also taught me the value of hard work. When I used to complain about having to clean the fowl runs, she would hug me and say, "Hayi, togo sisi ungafi. Cleaning the fowl runs and collecting eggs is work suitable for young girls like you. When you are older you will do even harder work according to your ability and age. Just look forward to the weekend, when you will get your fair share of eating eggs." When she said that, I had to smile. As a young girl who had not yet started her menstrual cycle I was allowed to eat eggs, but tradition forbade Olga from eating these dangerous aphrodisiacs. Imagine that! Nowadays you would be laughed at.

For a long time I felt adrift, but the constant routine of my new home served to calm my insecurities. I had promised Mama that I would strive to become the person I wanted to be. I knew I had to learn to deal with fear, which is little more than the dark room where negatives are developed. And I succeeded.

After some time I started enjoying my life at Mamkhulu's. I began again to feel warmth in my heart, and I learnt to enjoy helping out where necessary. Having two of my brothers with me at Mamkhulu's was a blessing. It made me sad that Sipho couldn't be there with us, but he was so much older than me, already living his own life. I guess he must also have been lonely, though, because when he turned eighteen a few months after Pila and I moved to Zazulwana, he joined Sobantu in the army.

Despite her sometimes military discipline and mutterings of dissent in the children's ranks, Mamkhulu always tried to maintain the peace and create a happy, loving atmosphere in the home. Her strong religious beliefs and family values provided the solid foundation for us to grow up.

Mamkhulu was a good woman; I say this not because Mamkhulu was my mother's sister, but because it is the truth. Yes, she was strict and a stickler for rules, but she had a good heart and her rules provided us with security. She loved the children that were entrusted in her care. She would always reward good behaviour with open praise or some extra meat or pudding. I know she was driven by a deep desire to help us grow into competent and responsible adults and citizens. We learnt to be strong and persevere. We learnt to be accountable for our actions.

Many years later, when I was a mother to six children of my own, I would think about Mamkhulu and what she did for me and the other children in her care. A patient and understanding adult plays such an important role in a child's growth and development on their way to independence. Mamkhulu taught me the value of running a functional, peaceful and happy home. Above all else, she taught me the importance of planning. In everything I have done, the one principle I have followed is not to do anything without proper planning.

The July after my father's death I enrolled at Zazulwana Primary School. This school was far bigger than the school in Manzimdaka, which was really just a farming school. Zazulwana had actual classrooms with rows and rows of desks and chairs for all the years except Sub A and B, which only had benches. The Lower Primary had two female teachers, one of them being Latiwe. The Higher Primary had four male teachers, including Mr Plumer Sbozo Ndwandwa, the principal.

It is normal for newcomers to be treated badly at school, but by the time we joined the bullying was over and we got a warm welcome from Sandie's friends. This is possibly because Sandie would otherwise have put them in their place, as we discovered when one boy said to Sandie, talking about Pila and me, "Hey, Sandie! Are these two your brothers? They look just like you."

Sandie was offended because his sister had been called a boy and got into a fight with the boy after school. Fortunately, none of the teachers noticed. Latiwe heard about the incident, though, and made Sandie carry her briefcase for the whole week instead of rotating it between the children from Mamkhulu's house.

Every month, without fail, Mama sent postal orders to Mamkhulu to pay our school fees. Whenever possible, she would send beautiful second-hand clothes for all of us. And at the end of that first year, towards Christmas, she came home.

We waited for her at the Butterworth train station – Sandie, Pila and me. She was very smartly dressed when she stepped off the train, only to be bowled over by her three children. We were so happy to see her, everyone crying and hugging. Then Pila asked, in happy innocence, "Where's Daddy? Is he with you?"

Mama turned away, but not before I saw the tears roll down her cheeks. She stood that way for a few minutes, struggling for control of herself. Then she turned back and explained to Pila that he was dead and wasn't going to come back. Sandie apologised on Pila's behalf, but it wasn't necessary. Mama was back to being happy to see us all.

The Christmas dinner Mama cooked was superb. We enjoyed her new cooking skills. The Christmas cake and pudding she made were out of this world. Mama had bought small gifts for everyone – facecloths, handkerchiefs, balls and so on – so all the children were happy. A sheep was slaughtered to celebrate the good school performance of all the children who had passed that year. Mama was very happy to see that we were learning and doing well at school. One of the reasons I did so well at school was because of Latiwe. In the evenings she would give generously of her time to help us children with our homework. Latiwe motivated me to work hard and do well.

Too soon, Mama had to go back to Johannesburg and we returned to school. After my first summer at Mamkhulu's, and for every summer after that, Mama arranged for sorghum, wheat and potatoes to be railed from Cala to Butterworth after the harvest. Mamkhulu, herself born in Cala, valued these crops for their quality. Seeing the joy on the children's faces as they watched bags and bags of food being delivered made me feel so proud of my Mama.

Nogusha was less pleased with the bounty. "They are also harvesting in Tsomo," she said. "Why doesn't my father send us something too?" I could read the disappointment on her face. "Never mind," I said, trying to comfort her. "Mama loves all the children at Mamkhulu's house. That is why she has sent all this food. It's for all of us."

Years passed. Finally the day came when I finished Standard Six with a first-class pass. My good marks were my ticket to the prestigious Healdtown High and Training College in Fort Beaufort. It was every Xhosa-speaking child's aim to go to Healdtown. It was the school to be in, producing students who would later become leaders in the African community. Oliver Tambo was one such student. The list is endless. I felt so proud of myself that if you could measure happiness by the number of stars, I would have filled so many bags you would need a wagon to carry them.

# 4

The intricate preparations for going to boarding school started immediately after Christmas. Nogate, Mamkhulu's daughter-in-law, who was a dressmaker, sewed many of the items I needed. Mama sent the rest of the stuff from Johannesburg, most of it second-hand. All my belongings were marked with my name and cleaned, ironed and neatly packed in a brand new trunk. For the first time I had my own sheets, towels, facecloth, slippers and nightgown. Even my shoes were brand new. I could not sleep for days, I was so excited.

At last the day dawned when I was to leave for school. The thought that I was going to make the journey by train made me feel dizzy. I had seen pictures of trains, but it was quite a revelation to learn that they need special rails to move.

Sandie and Mpondo carried my trunk the six kilometres to Butterworth train station. Two of the girls from Mamkhulu's house came with to help me carry the lighter things. The station was full of boys and girls, chatting and greeting each other. To me it seemed as though they all knew each other. There were trunks and baskets of food wherever you looked.

Latiwe had organised Nondlela Bikitsha, a senior student from Healdtown who came from Zazulwana village, to take care of me on my journey. She called out my name, checked my belongings and train tickets, and then told some boys to help me carry my luggage.

We slowly climbed on the train. It was long, with many carriages. Students walked up and down the narrow passage, banging into each other with their big trunks. Each compartment was big enough for six students with their luggage placed on overhead racks. The train was filled with smoke and a nasty smell from the burning coal and the students smoking in the passage. I found a place and stood at the open window to chat to Sandie and Mpondo and the rest of them.

I noticed a couple of young girls glancing at me. "Perhaps they're new too," said Nondlela. She was right. Later the same day I got a chance to talk to these girls at the Healdtown Girls' Hostel. Two of them – Rachel Nomazotsho Nzo and Nomabhaso Dumse – became my close friends for many years. The train stopped at Alice train station. Dozens of students piled out, on their way to Lovedale High and Teacher's Training School. Others were on their way to Fort Hare University. When we got to Fort Beaufort station, a big bus was already waiting to transport us to Healdtown. About eighty of us climbed on that bus, so many more than the handful I thought we would be. The boys helped the girls with their heavy trunks and baskets. This was the first time that I realised that my knowledge of the world had been limited by my environment.

At Healdtown the hostels were all named after previous principals, who were of English descent. It was therefore not surprising at all, that the educational system and the mode of life were all based on the English model. This is the reason that many Xhosa households, many homes in other parts of the country that have been influenced by missionaries, follow a westernised type of life. There was insistence on western concepts of cooking, house organisation and management.

The weekday boarding-school routine would have seemed quite daunting had life at Mamkhulu's not prepared me for the discipline of waking up at a fixed time, always getting dressed in the prescribed uniform, doing my chores, being attentive in class and always being well behaved. I quickly fell into step.

Sundays were mostly spent studying, relaxing and looking forward to the special Sunday meal with the bread pudding dessert. In the mornings we went to church. Mr Mokitini, the boarding master, would lead us in prayer and Reverend Arthur Wellington, the school principal at the time, would deliver a sermon. Dr Wellington was a very kind person who saw the humanity in everyone, of all colours.

He treated everyone with respect and dignity. When he died in 1946, he was buried in the local African cemetery, according to his wishes.

Coming from a Christian home, I enjoyed church. Confirmation and taking my first Holy Communion were very significant moments in my life. Faith in God has been a stepping stone in my life and that of my children. It is my firm belief that each one of us needs the presence of the divine. When we are facing challenging times or even when we are happy, it is good to begin and end the day by acknowledging the spirit within us.

Soon after I arrived at Healdtown, people started teasing me about my height and clothes. I was tall for a girl, and my gym dress was easily identifiable as being homemade because the pleats were not as deep as those bought from a uniform outfitter. I wrote to Olga about this teasing, as I wrote to her about everything in my life. She wrote back quickly: "Don't worry about it. Be proud of your height. Carry yourself like a queen."

One day I was standing at the tuckshop, hands in my blazer pockets, when a group of girls walked up to me. "Hey, newcomer," said one. "Why are you wearing an old blazer even though you're new? Is it second-hand?"

The rest of the girls roared with laughter. I remembered my sister's words of encouragement and gathered my spirit, stretching my frame taller and leaning towards her so she could see my nose flare. "Yes!" I replied. "It is second-hand. What are you going to do about it?"

This was not the only time I was the subject of ridicule. It might have left me in tears if I didn't have Olga as the rock in my life. Even though she was so far away, I carried her in my heart and my mind. She taught me to stand up for myself, but also to have empathy and patience for those who bullied me.

At school there was a bench outside the principal's office where those who were being sent home because they owed school fees sat. It always struck me as odd that it was often the best-dressed girls, the ones who could spend lots of money at the tuckshop, who sat on this bench. I wondered why parents would send loads of pocket money to their children before sending school fees. Parents today are the same, bending over backwards to provide their children with the frills instead of giving them what they really need – reassurance that they are loved.

When my mother occasionally sent me pocket money, I would save it and ask her to add on to the money she had when I took the train to Johannesburg to visit her and Aunt Violet during the winter holidays. My mother worked for one Mrs Robertson and Violet worked for another, right next door. Both the Robertsons were very wealthy. Looking back, I guess the two Robertson families must have been related, because the servants' quarters where my mother and her sister lived were right next to each other, divided only by a verandah that had been converted into a living room for them both.

It was during one such visit that the Mrs Robertson my mother worked for invited me to sit with her on the main house's verandah and chat. When I first started visiting my mother, I was reluctant to talk to Mrs Robertson because I was shy about my English, although she was always very pleasant to me. But this was in Standard Nine. I had been at Healdtown for three years and was ready to take a seat.

"Tell me, Connie," said Mrs Robertson. "What do you want to be when you leave school?"

"A lawyer, Mrs Robertson," I said. "I just don't know how to go about it."

A shadow crossed her face. "Are you sure? University is very expensive, you know."

I hadn't realised that it would cost us for me to study law. I didn't know what to say, so I didn't say anything.

Mrs Robertson sat forward. "What about nursing?" she suggested, her voice gentle. "Nursing is a good job to have. A good job, and an important job. And you won't have to pay to study, which might help your mother now that your younger brother will also be going to high school next year."

I thought about Olga, who had completed her teacher's training and moved to the Transvaal to study nursing. As far as I knew, there were only four other career paths open to me as a young African: teacher, clerk, priest and police officer. The more I thought about it, the more I preferred the idea of caring for the sick to defending those who had broken the law.

By now the Second World War had been over for a year. Sobantu, Sipho and Sandie, who had also joined the army when he turned eighteen, had come home, although Sipho and Sandie were extremely frail. Sandie went to Welkom and Sipho moved to Cape Town, where he had a daughter with his girlfriend, before moving back to Cala, where he died towards the end of 1948.

Perhaps I was inspired by his death to pursue a career in nursing. I received my junior certificate a year later, again with flying colours, and I applied to study at Coronation Hospital the following year. It was 1948, I was nineteen years old and the only thought in my head was, "Johannesburg, here I come".

# 5

The moment I saw Coronation hospital, I loved it. It was one of the three big hospitals in Johannesburg at the time. Unlike Johannesburg General and Baragwanath, which sprawled across many buildings, Coronation was a well-built, compact red-brick building surrounded by parking lots and flowers and trees. It still looked new back then.

Going up the steps to the main entrance, visitors were met by long passages running off to the left and the right. To the left were the doctors' offices and the main kitchen; to the right was the entrance to the casualty ward. Everything was well arranged and very neat. There were four wards on each of the four floors and the operating theatres were upstairs.

Casualty at Coronation was always very busy, because the hospital served the coloured people who lived in Coronationville, the Indian people who lived in Westbury, and the African people who lived in the Western Native Township and Sophiatown. Segregation was alive for the well, but less so for the sick.

Outside, down a little path, was another big building housing the nurses' home and lecture rooms. Trainee nurses were given free accommodation upstairs at the nurses' home. Each trainee shared a room split in two by wardrobes. We were given everything we needed – linen, towels, even red uniforms with crisply starched white aprons and a broad white belt that tied at the waist.

My first day at Coronation Hospital was incredibly exciting. I was one of twelve new trainees. Some were dressed simply, like me, while others wore smart clothes. We started talking and I learnt that some of the trainees had had to wait a long time to be accepted to nursing school. I had registered to apply the previous December, submitted the completed application forms by February and was told that I could start working by May. I suspect having references from the Robertsons helped me get in.

A woman came and led us to a smaller lounge, where she gave us each a batch of documents to read. She walked with a confident stride that made me think of a soldier. She introduced herself and explained how uniforms denote position among the nursing staff. Her uniform indicated that she was an assistant matron.

Olga had told me that junior nurses mostly worked in the sluice rooms, washing dirty sheets and hospital gowns. I was sent to the sluice room in the children's ward. All the trainee nurses worked the same number of hours, albeit at different times. Seeing my name at the bottom of the off-duty list gave me a sense of belonging.

At first I felt discouraged at washing soiled nappies all day, but then I realised that all trainee nurses started here. Now it was my turn. How could I wish for special treatment? Thinking like this gave me the courage I would need to become a nurse and do what was expected of me, properly.

The work was hard, but I was smart and eager. At the end of one long, busy day I remember thinking that nursing was not for anyone who didn't have strong legs. Some days it felt as though I did nothing but walk up and down those long corridors, from ward to ward. It was tiring, to tell the truth.

Fortunately, I have always been blessed with long, strong legs. I could take it. Every morning, I got up with renewed determination and every evening I went to bed with an extreme feeling of satisfaction. I felt physically and emotionally empowered, and was learning to relax and accept life not as a series of challenges but as a joyous journey to awakening. This was nursing college not boarding school. I settled in quickly, feeling more assured every day that nursing was indeed the profession for me. My earlier desire to be a lawyer was forgotten.

When I was off duty, I would visit Mama and Violet at work. In those days the trams still ran. I would catch the tram from Sophiatown to Johannesburg central, then catch the whites-only bus to Melrose Street, sitting in the back where Africans were allowed. In all, it took me about an hour to get there.

By this time, Olga was a nurse at Johannesburg General Hospital. I would often arrive at Mama's to find her already there, having tea with Mama and Violet in one of their kitchens. We would then share a wonderful time of togetherness spoilt only by the memory of family members still left in the Cape. Sometimes Olga stayed there overnight. I would have loved to do the same, but I wasn't allowed to sleep out as a trainee nurse.

During these visits I would ask Mama and Violet questions about my life and family when I was growing up. Olga also took an interest in this topic and would write down what they spoke about when I wasn't there so that I wouldn't miss out. I kept these notes for many years.

I had passed my first year and was about to start my second when we were told that trainee nurses would no longer receive free accommodation. I didn't know what to do. It was impossible to find suitable accommodation for a single, young African woman in those days. Many student nurses, especially those from the Cape, had to pack their bags and go home.

I was not to be deterred. Steeling myself, I applied to other training hospitals throughout the country. One of my applications went to Frere Hospital in East London. A few weeks later I was back in my home province, training to be a nurse once more. Only later did I discover how important this move would be in altering the course of my life.

Apart from Cecilia Makhiwane Hospital in Mdantsane, Frere Hospital was the only government hospital serving the African and coloured communities in the area. The next big hospital was in Port Elizabeth, 240 kilometres away.

Frere Hospital was a disappointment. Whereas Coronation was compact and purpose-built, Frere was scattered and lacked uniformity. It was as though the buildings had been built for some other purpose. Casualty and some other wards were at the front of the complex, while the nurses' home and lecture rooms were at the back.

I was immediately placed on night duty with Nomabhaso, my old high-school friend who had also transferred from Coronation Hospital. One thing that struck me about Frere was that the hospital staff consisted of whites as well as Africans. At Coronation, there were only African staff members.

One night, an elderly white porter came to help us with a restless patient in our ward. The patient kept getting up and trying to run away. We needed someone strong to help handcuff him to the bed, for his own good. We had managed to secure the handcuff around the patient's wrist when he pulled free and ran down the passage. The porter ran after him, yelling incomprehensibly.

What we didn't realise until later was that the patient had used the handcuffs to chain himself to the porter, who was actually being dragged along. His incomprehensible shouts were actually cries for help. No one understood what was happening until some white ambulance drivers stopped the patient near the entrance. The porter had to be treated for shock and we nurses had to write statements about the incident to explain our "carelessness".

A few months after I started training at Frere, I received the news that Mama's health was failing. She had a painful lump in her breast and grew tired easily. That Easter, Mrs Robertson sent her home to Cala to rest. I was distressed at the news but thankful that my life had brought me closer to home. Cala was just a few hours away by bus. I would be able to visit her often.

Meanwhile, life went on. I immersed myself in my studies and, in my spare time, took ballroom dancing lessons at the community hall in Duncan Village. Ballroom dancing was very popular at the time, and many nurses took it up. Some even danced professionally. My first few lessons I watched the other dancers, fascinated. The more I watched, the more I realised that I really liked dancing. I started understanding the moves. Soon I was as absorbed in dancing as I was in my studies, devoting all my spare time to perfecting my steps. My height, the curse of my school years, made it easier for me to master the intricate and graceful moves.

There was this one tall dancing instructor, Sol, who grew up in Butterworth. We always spoke about him back at the nurses' residence – how handsome and graceful he was, what a catch he would be, each girl competing with the next to prove that she knew him better. He was a good-looking man, no doubt. Elegant on the dance floor. When he took my hand to instruct me, I could never resist smelling his shaven skin. He reminded me so much of my father, always clean and smelling like bath soap. And when we danced together, it was like our bodies had been built to fit into each other. We were both tall and slim. Sol would hold me very close and murmur in my ear. I felt at ease with him. He was so warm. We both loved the foxtrot. Together, we were a work of art, swishing and swaying across the dance floor.

Sol worked as a postal clerk, which might explain why the local post office was always a hive of activity, with nurses posting letters and sending money orders home. I was among those who enjoyed these postal errands.

When Sol found out I had also grown up in Butterworth, he showed a great deal of interest in me. One day, he asked me to meet him at the post office during lunchtime. He would also be free. I was so excited. It felt as though there were butterflies in my stomach. Eventually the day came. I went to the hospital kiosk to buy a sandwich and a drink to take with. I did not know what Sol had in mind for us at the post office, but I knew the shops were far from his office.

I got to the post office before it closed for lunch. Eventually the last customers left and the door clicked behind me, locking us in together. We sat in his office, away from the counters. When I was growing up, the girls at school would joke about what we would say if we ever found out that a man liked us. "Tell him to bring me a goat because I am a cabbage," we would laugh. On that day, it happened to me – only Sol was the goat, and he could spare no cabbage.

Soon it was 2 pm. Sol had to open the doors for the customers and I had to get back to the hospital. I forgot all about my sandwich when I left. From that day on I was a regular customer at the post office, but only during lunchtime. I realised I was falling in love with my instructor. I asked around and was delighted to learn that he was not in a relationship.

From time to time different dance groups would gather at the community hall to compete and demonstrate their ballroom-dancing skills. During these events, beginners were only given the chance to dance during the jive sessions, when the formal rhythms of the waltz and cha-cha gave way to the modern rhythm of jive songs, to which professionals and amateurs alike could dance. Everyone loved these sessions, and most people took the opportunity to dance to them. It created the most wonderful feeling of togetherness.

As soon as the dance music started, Sol would be the first to take to the floor, dancing smoothly alone for some minutes before the other professionals would pick their partners and join him. This was always a nerve-wracking moment for the best female dancers, who would sit anxiously, wondering whether they would be chosen. Sol, the dancing instructor, would be the last to pick. He would take my hand and say, a smile in his voice, "May I please have this dance, Miss Beginner?"

By now it was clear to everyone who cared to know that the friendship between us had developed into something more. Some of the nurses that I stayed with took it upon themselves to warn me about this professional dancer of mine. They suspected he was not a serious-minded man. "He's nothing more than a charmer," they said. "He makes the ladies fall in love with him and then he drops them, just like that."

When I was a child washing clothes in the river, the water always made such a noise that we had to shout to be heard. That was how I viewed these warnings, like the noise of water – to be ignored. I drew my confidence from the fact that Sol had opened up to me earlier, telling me how, when he became associated with beautiful lady dancers, he always took care to keep the involvement short in case they misinterpreted his attentions. I accepted his explanation and was greatly relieved that he had opened up to me because by then I was madly in love with him.

Sol, I learnt, had also gone to school in Butterworth. When he completed his Standard Six, he was awarded a bursary to study at Lovedale High and Teacher's College. The bursary was a blessing, as his mother was unable to pay for his studies after Standard Six, although she always made sure she provided him with all the other necessities. His story was so similar to mine, and still fills me with awe for all the mothers in the country who have raised their children in difficult times through sacrifice and hard work.

When he was a little older, Sol played golf. He started off as a caddy, carrying golf bags to earn some pocket money – the beginnings of an entrepreneur were evident even then – which he saved up to buy a bicycle to ride to school and to visit his mother. In those days, only privileged children owned a bicycle. This was part of the reason I trusted him so. He could have used the money to buy cigarettes, sunglasses, takeaway food. He chose not to. To me, his actions spoke of a man with values, the kind of man who would use his talents wisely and fruitfully.

After completing his education at Lovedale, he briefly lived in Cape Town and Port Elizabeth before landing a job as a government clerk, which gave him the opportunity to be allocated a house. In those days, Africans could not buy land or own houses. Whatever homes we had, especially in urban areas, we lived in at the mercy of the municipality, paying monthly rent for the accommodation.

In 1948 he joined the post office as a clerk in a small office in Port Elizabeth. He also joined the ANC, a move that would eventually contribute towards my own political awakening. Before I met Sol, I belonged to the Youth League without really knowing what it stood for. It was only after I met him that I started going to meetings, marches and mass funerals, and gaining a true understanding of South Africa's problems. Towards the end of 1949, Sol was transferred to a bigger post office in Duncan Village. This is where he worked when I met him.

Sol used his position at work and his role as a dance instructor to develop good values and habits in the young adults around him. He wanted those he worked with and taught to be people of stature;

to have vision and ambition. He believed that all men and women should contribute to the growth and well-being of their community. In acting out this belief, he proudly displayed his dancing abilities, great sense of humour and captivating smile.

Early one Saturday evening, after dancing practice, as Sol escorted me back to the nurses' home, he said to me, "This afternoon I visited a flower shop and spoke openly to the owner, an elderly lady."

I waited for him to keep talking, but instead he took out a small parcel from his inner jacket pocket. He unfolded a silky-soft tissue with two red flowers in it – a rose and a carnation. He placed the rose in my palm and said, "Manse, this rose is a symbol of my love for you. And this" – he put the carnation in my hand – "is my heart. Always keep them safely together."

My heart beat faster than a racehorse's hooves. I couldn't see properly and felt faint. I had to lean on the front door of the nurses' home for a few minutes, just to regain my composure. When next I looked, he was gone.

# 6

By the end of 1950 I had passed my second-year exams and had one year left to complete my training. I was in love with my dance instructor. Mama's health was the only darkness in my life. At Cala they had treated her sore breast until it burst open. It was only then that they diagnosed breast cancer.

By now she had been living at home for more than eight months. At the beginning of December 1950, I went to Cala to visit her, my mind full of plans to organise a party for her sixtieth birthday later in the month. When I got there I was shocked to see how her condition had deteriorated. She looked tired. She tried her best to be cheerful, but not even the medication could keep the pain away for very long. She had lost a lot of weight. It was difficult to see Mama – this tall, smart woman – suffering.

My fear of being separated from her grew very real. Although I had taken care of very ill patients who had managed to recover and go home, this was different. Nothing I had been confronted with at the hospital prepared me for seeing Mama like this. I admit, I was selfish. Instead of giving her a chance to sleep when the painkillers gave her some short relief, I made her talk to me instead.

"All that happens in life today will be history tomorrow," she said one day. "What is important is to be grateful to God for today's moment. This can unlock the fullness of life tomorrow." She then told me that it was important to be thankful to Mamkhulu for all that she had done for us. She told us to care for each other, Pila and myself. She made me promise to always value education.

She said all this in short bursts, her sentences broken by the drugs and the pain. I gathered up her words and thanked her for them. I thanked her for everything she had done for us children, and promised to fulfil her wishes. "I must still get you a birthday present," I said.

She just gave a small nod and smiled.

I went back to Frere to work. Olga took leave and went home to nurse Mama. Seven days later, I was called to the matron's office.

At Frere Hospital the managers' offices were viewed as sacred, a place of fear. Usually, when you were summoned to the matron's office, you were about to be warned about a serious offence or expelled.

When I got to the matron's half-open door I rolled down my sleeves, knocked, walked in and introduced myself, as was nursing etiquette. The matron's office had big windows with expensive curtains running from ceiling to floor; behind her was a bookshelf full of neatly arranged books and files.

Normally, the matron would straighten up and look a person in the eye when they walked in, as though she could read the truth there. This time, she sat still behind her oversized desk, frowning at the pen she was tapping against her blotting pad. "How old are you, nurse?" she asked. "When last did you see your mother?"

"I'm twenty-one years old, Matron," I replied. "I saw my mother last week."

Finally she looked at me, her expression a little more kind. "I'm sorry," she said, handing over a pink telegram envelope. "Your mother died yesterday."

I buried my face in my hands, sobbing from deep down in my belly. I thought the matron was still talking when my ward sister came in, gave me a hug and steered me out of the office. In retrospect, I think the matron had asked her to be there to get me out of her office as quickly as possible.

I had lost forever the most important piece in my puzzle of life. A sharp pain tore at my heart as I imagined Mama in the setting of death, a mound of rocky, freshly dug soil on top of a coffin with her motionless but very precious body. Never again would I hug Mama or write her a letter. I was grateful that I had been able to thank her for her selflessness after my father's death. Were it not for her, where would I have been? How I wished she could have been given good health to witness the next step in my life, now that I had found Sol. The woman who had brought me into this world was gone. What an irreplaceable loss.

Mama's funeral passed in a blur. Afterwards, we were told that the mourning period was to be six months, during which time we were to wear black clothes. In the first weekend in June we would gather to hold a cleansing ceremony, where we would burn black buttons from our mourning clothes. After that, we could wear normal clothes again. The loss of Mama disturbed my faith for some time – but the gain of a loving, understanding man gave me strength not to lose hope. Eventually, my grief crystallised into a burning desire to make Mama proud, even in death, and to use the talents given to me to the best of my ability.

Shortly after Mama's death I started gaining weight. At first I thought it was because I was under less pressure from work and studies, but the worrying thing was that even since before Mama's death I had been feeling nauseous and generally weak. I finally buckled and went to see a doctor. I was surprised when the doctor said I was four months pregnant.

When he found out, Sol held me close and said, "Don't worry, Manse. I will never abandon you. Perhaps having a baby is not a bad idea after all." But I worried I wasn't ready to have a baby yet. I felt angry with him and sorry for myself. I burst into tears. Sol looked confused. "Why are you crying? We have already talked about getting married."

That wasn't what was upsetting me. I was devastated at the thought that I might never become a nurse, that I would never get to enjoy my independence and be able to do what I liked. I wanted to get married, but only later. Sol and I had already discussed our future but had postponed concrete plans. We wanted our path to be sturdy, but sure. Finding out I was pregnant so soon after Mama's death was a blow.

But I trusted Sol and I believed in him, because I loved him. I thought of what my mother would have said, of what Olga would say. She would be so disappointed at our carelessness. There was so much explaining to do, but Sol was there all the time.

Culturally, pregnancy out of wedlock was a disgrace. We would have to get married to save us from the embarrassment. Sol went to arrange lobola with Uncle Elliot, who said that we would have to wait before arranging the wedding as my family was still in mourning for Mama.

I told the hospital matron about what had happened. She had a lot to say about the importance of self-respect and so on, but told me to "go ahead with my plans" and come back in three weeks' time. I suppose she meant I had to get married, so that my pregnancy could be recognised, but with my family in mourning that could not happen. By the end of the three weeks there was nothing to report. The matron was understanding, but there was nothing she could do to help me. I was suspended from lectures and told to leave the nurses' home until the situation changed.

We had no other choice but to find a place for me to live. I couldn't stay with Sol because, Uncle Elliot told us, it was culturally forbidden to live together before marriage. He sounded frankly irritated at the suggestion. Cala was out of question because there were no antenatal clinics or hospitals nearby. So we turned to the person who had taken me in under difficult circumstances before.

Mamkhulu welcomed me with sympathy. She kindly allowed Sol to visit me at her home, provided the visits were kept private. By now I was eight months pregnant. After two weeks, Mamkhulu took me to the antenatal clinic at Butterworth Hospital. The clinic staff reprimanded me for coming late, telling me that I should be coming for weekly check-ups at this late stage in my pregnancy. When I went back a week later, they suggested I should be admitted, because Zazulwana to the hospital was a long distance for a pregnant woman to travel. Two days later, on the morning of 7 April 1951, I gave birth to our first son, Tammie. Sol came through that afternoon. We were so happy and proud of our healthy baby boy.

As was her way, Mamkhulu took charge of everything after that. She even tried to monopolise the baby, trying to fill the gap left by Mama. Being from Butterworth, she knew Sol's mother, and set about making arrangements.

Shortly after the cleansing ceremony in June, my clan was ready to meet Sol's clan to arrange our union. First Sol had to pay damages for making me pregnant. Then he had to pay lobola to marry me. Sol became my greatest gift in my hour of greatest despair. He fulfilled his responsibilities and finally we received permission to get married.

But that was not the last of our obstacles. When Mamkhulu met the church elders of the Methodist church in Zazulwana, to which I belonged, they told her that pregnancy out of wedlock was a religious violation and I had been demoted. It would take a year of confirmation courses before I could be reconfirmed as a full member of the church again.

This seemed unnecessarily complicated to us. All we wanted was a meaningful, spiritual church wedding. Then a cousin's colleague introduced us to the African Methodist Episcopal Church. We paid our registration fees and we were accepted as members. Sol requested that the banns of marriage be announced for three successive Sundays. These banns were there to make sure that there were no legal or moral obstacles to our getting married – a previous marriage, for instance, or an underage partner without parental consent. Of course there weren't, and finally we were free to say our vows.

The ceremony was to take place in East London. A few days before, I unofficially moved back into the nurse's home, from where I could help arrange our private wedding and a small celebration afterwards.

Sol and I took a taxi to a jewellery store in the city to buy the rings we had picked out earlier. It was July 1951, the end of winter.

As we walked back to the taxis, it started pouring with rain. I got completely soaked. We had to buy me new clothes at Garlicks and stuff my wet clothes into Sol's briefcase.

When we got back to Sol's place, we found our friends had gathered there to help us celebrate buying our rings. One nurse greeted us, "Hello Sol! Where's Connie? How can you dump her for this lady now?" Another chimed in, "Sol's a charmer. He picks up women easily." We all laughed at that.

Finally, 2 August arrived. Our wedding day. At the church were some of our colleagues, Sol's two sisters and a cousin from Butterworth, Olga and my younger brother Pila, both from Johannesburg, and my elder brother, Sobantu, and Uncle Elliot. The reverend performed the ceremony in the church vestry. "May God give His grace abundantly to this couple, and may peace be all around them in their future, forever," said the reverend. For some reason I wrote down those words in my pocket book; to my mind they were special. When Sol was in a teasing mood he would quote them. After the ceremony, our friends planned a small party to celebrate with us.

After our wedding, we went to live at Sol's family home in Butterworth, where we had a traditional marriage ceremony. This ceremony took place after sunset, with elders from both our families present. The ritual was a simple one: I sat behind a door on a floor mat next to my sister-in-law and ate a special piece of meat and drank a glass of sour milk. This was called "ukutyiswa amasi", or the drinking of sour milk. Elders from both sides of the family then gave me words of wisdom and encouragement as I embarked on this new phase in my life. After the ceremony, I was to be addressed by my clan name, Mahlongwane, as "makoti", the bride, or, as "molokazana", meaning daughter-in-law.

After the "ukutyiswa amasi" ceremony I was not sure what to do in my new home. Sol was busy with the other men near the kraal. My sisters-in-law were both married with young children, so they were getting ready to go back home. Fortunately, my mother-in-law had taken a month's leave from her job as a domestic worker in Butterworth to stay at home for the first few weeks while I was a makoti.

I was very grateful to her for being around when I needed her, and we soon developed a strong bond. She guided me like a mother and I tried to do my best as a makoti. I wore my new traditional dresses, a black doek low over my forehead and a scarf over my shoulders. I even carried my baby on my back a few times. Sol was happy to see us chatting together. He was close to his mother and I was happy to share in that warm bond with him.

Usually, a bride would serve as a makoti for four months before she became a young wife, after which she was allowed to wear a headscarf of any colour, worn away from the eyes, and to replace the shawl with a scarf around the waist. I had been a makoti for only three weeks when I received a letter. Uncle Elliot had taken our marriage certificate to the matron. My suspension had been lifted. I was allowed to resume training at Frere Hospital, but as a live-out student nurse because of the baby. I moved into Sol's place in Duncan Village and finally resumed my life as a trainee nurse.

Sol rented one room in a two-roomed semi-detached house. We shared a toilet, a shower and a water tap with the other occupant, an elderly policeman whose family lived in the country. We were fortunate to be in such a small house. In Duncan Village there were many large houses made of wood and iron with ten to twelve rooms, owned by landlords who rented out the rooms to a family per room. These people lived on top of each other, everyone sharing a common toilet and water tap.

One day, we noticed a woman visiting our housemate. "Just a woman looking for a job," our neighbour told Sol, but we later found out it was his mistress.

We organised a cot and everything we needed to take care of Tammie. He was already eating solids and being bottle-fed. We offered the neighbour's mistress a job as a nanny, since she was always at our place anyway. She took the position immediately. She looked after him while I was working during the day, and during the night Tammie was with me. He was a very happy boy.

Six months later, by March 1952, Tammie was almost a year old and very keen to play. It soon became clear to us that Sol's house and the surrounding area was not suitable for a child to play because of hard shrubbery and stones. We shared this concern with Mamkhulu. Fortunately for us, she had just been thinking about my upcoming exams and was worried that I would not have enough time to study. Tammie went to live with his great-aunt, Mamkhulu, who had already helped me so much in my life. My boy was very happy at Mamkhulu's. He had friends to play with and the environment was clean and safe for him to play freely. He was so settled there by the time I passed my exams that we decided to let him stay at Mamkhulu's when I took a contract position at Frere Hospital. My career as a professional nurse had begun.

# 7

---

I first experienced the barbarity of apartheid in November 1952, about the time I registered as a state nurse. It was a Sunday afternoon. I was looking forward to the end of my shift at 4.30 pm. Suddenly, there was a call on the intercom. "Emergency. Emergency in casualty. Please, everyone come."

We left one nurse in the ward to watch the patients and rushed to casualty. What was usually a well-ordered unit was in utter chaos. There was blood everywhere, injured people groaning and pleading for help. They lay on stretchers, benches, wheelchairs, even on the floor, and still more ambulance drivers were pushing their way in with heavy stretchers. The injured threw up all over the place, probably from the teargas. The smell of vomit and beer made my throat clench.

Dozens of friends and family members anxiously pushed into the crowd, hoping to identify those on the floor. The police were there too, pulling people aside, asking questions, threatening, trying to find the ringleaders of what they called a riot.

My head reeling, I picked my way over bodies of people who were already dead, but had to be certified by a doctor before they could be removed, and started helping the doctors. It was heartbreaking to see innocent people so badly wounded. Some were confused, asking questions. Some still clutched their Bibles, fresh from church. What traumatised me the most, though, was seeing extreme hatred and anger on some of the white doctors' and nurses' faces as they manhandled the injured as if they were rags.

Where is their compassion? I wondered. Where are their ethics? I couldn't understand how they could despise their fellow South Africans so much even as they removed bullets and stitched up wounds. Some of the injured had been shot in the head and the back. If they survived, they would probably be permanently crippled or paralysed.

One young man came in clutching his eye and yelling with pain. He refused to take his hand away until he had to be given a pain injection. When I finally pried it away, my heart sank to see his eye almost hanging sideways. I lost hope that he would ever see again, young as he was. He was immediately rushed off to the operating theatre. I never saw him again.

We worked through the night, treating the injured and making them as comfortable as possible. But it was clear to me that many of them would be permanently disfigured. It was equally clear that these people had done nothing wrong to deserve such terrible treatment.

By early the following morning the chaos had subsided. I felt hungry, dirty, tired. We were busy tidying up when we noticed some freshly dressed visitors inquiring about their loved ones. Not the injured this time, but those who had gone to work and not come home. I had come on duty at 7 am on Sunday. It was now 6.30 am on Monday.

Sol was one of these visitors. He seemed shocked to see wounded patients still lying around, either waiting to be discharged or admitted to the wards. "I tried to come through during the night," he said. "The police had put up a barricade. I decided to go home and try again in the morning." He was very relieved to see me.

On our way home I told Sol I did not know what the crowd had been protesting against. I suspected it could have been the Pass laws, but in truth it could have been anything. The security police never passed up on an opportunity to act mercilessly towards any suspicious crowd. It was as if they thought that killing unarmed people was the solution to the country's problems.

When we got home I told Sol everything I had seen and done in the casualty ward. It was as though I had to get the story out of me. It was too heavy for me to carry alone. He listened kindly and was sad to hear about the poor state of those injured. "I'm so proud of you for helping those protesters," he said. "You deserve some sort of recognition for serving your country. A medal."

I gave a tired laugh and rested my head against his shoulder. "But no one knew I was even there," I said. "It wasn't as though they took roll call or even knew who was on duty. Everyone just showed up and did what needed to be done."

By the morning many stories were going around. According to the newspapers, the crowd had been protesting against the murder of a nun who had done a lot to care for the sick in the vicinity of the Catholic church in Duncan Village. She had burnt to death, the newspapers said. But with politics one never knows the truth. The only truth that existed for me was that the apartheid system was unacceptable and that I had to be part of the effort to fight it.

# 8

From January 1953, I worked in the male ward in Frere Hospital under Sister Lewis. All professional nurses are called "sister". I knew I was good at my job – well organised, responsible and confident. I had received good reports during training, and was determined to maintain the high standards I had set myself in my first job as a professional nurse.

I succeeded in this goal. Not once was I called to the matron's office to defend my poor performance. The first and last time I was asked to explain myself was after the protest in November 1952, when those of us who had volunteered in casualty were asked to write reports about what had happened. I had commented in the report on the harsh treatment some of the other staff members gave patients and was ordered to rewrite it, which I did. In hindsight, I should have been more concerned at the fact that they did not give me the original report back.

Later, I went to the matron's office to plead for my requests to be considered. I had asked for a weekend off but Sister Lewis had turned me down repeatedly. It was my understanding that all newly trained nurses were entitled to a permanent position within six months of employment, motivated by good performance; to ask for a day off or a month off for annual leave as needed, and to be asked to be put on night duty when it was not their turn, if there was an acceptable reason. These benefits were given to us in writing; what wasn't on paper was that they applied only to white nurses.

The first time I approached the matron's office directly with my request, the assistant matron was the only one on duty. She settled the matter quickly by accepting both my requests. I was very thankful. The second time I approached the matron's office directly, the matron herself was there. She refused to overturn the ward sister's decision, saying I had no right to undermine Sister Lewis's authority.

After some months, it was my turn to be on night duty. I was pleased to finally be on this rotation because it was quieter than day duty. By now I suspected I was pregnant again, and welcomed the opportunity to rest.

On weekends, the sister in charge on night duty would sometimes ask me to escort her on her ward rounds, which took her down some deserted and dimly lit corridors. Normally, she would have been escorted by the night porter, but this was the weekend and there were no porters on duty.

I admit, I was curious to see what was happening on the "European" side of the hospital, as it was called in those days. I was always happy to oblige.

The first thing that struck me on these walks was the neatness in the passages and on entering the wards. There were chairs for patients and visitors to sit on and even a few pictures on the walls. On our side the wide corridors were very messy, littered with trolleys, wheelchairs, linen carriers and even oxygen cylinders, because there was no storage space for them. Visitors had to stand against the wall if they wanted to speak to a staff member.

One night, I caught a glimpse of the children's play area and was very impressed by what I saw. There were toys and books and lovely children's pictures hanging on the walls. The playroom on our side was disappointing by comparison. Boxes were piled one on top of the other. A few balls were scattered around with some half-torn newspapers.

I decided to dress up the playroom during my spare time. I shared my idea with some of my colleagues, asking if any of them were interested in helping. They all were. In a short space of time, that room was transformed into something beautiful. The children's ward staff was delighted and wrote to the night sister-in-charge to thank her. The night sister-in-charge forwarded the report to the matron, out of pride, I suspect. A few days later the matron issued a circular: "In future, if the night nurses have nothing to do, they should be taken off night duty instead of wasting their time."

My colleagues now regretted helping me. I felt guilty for getting them involved. I wrote an apology to the matron, letting her know that I had been the "ringleader". But I couldn't stop myself from adding, "We provided children with a sound base from which to develop their lives, like all other children in this same hospital."

Shortly after this, I gave Sister Lewis a letter from the doctor to let her know I was pregnant. I was only five months along, but knew that the central office would need a long notice to accommodate my absence on the roster. Sister Lewis took my letter to matron's office herself. All was quiet. Then, two months later, I received a notice that, although I had been working as a professional nurse for more than 15 months, I was not entitled to maternity leave as I was in a "contract position".

I went to the matron's office to appeal against the decision. I knocked, went inside and introduced myself. Before I could say anything, she snapped, "If I was you, I would forget about fighting this and just go. If you want to influence others so badly, perhaps you should have become a teacher."

I was astounded. Before I could say anything she told me to shut the door behind me. I left.

More and more it was becoming clear to me that politics had the power to disrupt my life. Sol and I began to talk seriously about needing to join the fight to defend our God-given colour. After all, we were being marginalised because of our Africanness.

I did not know what to do. Sister Lewis advised me to resign because, if I didn't and then went on maternity leave anyway, they would either label me as having absconded or I would be expelled and would lose any chance of ever working at any hospital again. I left at the end of March 1954.

By now Sol was a senior clerk at the post office, responsible for training staff throughout the Ciskei and Transkei. His job would take him away from home for four or five weeks at a time, three or four times a year. Fortunately, he was given a travel allowance that allowed him to visit home at the weekends.

Olga's husband, a church minister, had also been transferred – from Orlando in Johannesburg to a church in East London. Olga had found a job at the Duncan Village clinic, in the TB section. I was delighted to have my sister living close by again.

By now Sol and I rented a big one-roomed house with electricity and a big verandah where a child could play. Since I was no longer working, I had the time to look after Tammie. We went to fetch him from Mamkhulu's.

On 11 May, I went to the hospital to bring my new baby into the world. The next day, Sol came to visit me. I had a surprise waiting for him. Instead of one child, I presented him with two – twins, a boy and a girl, born a few hours apart. We named the boy Tembile Aubrey and the girl Tembise Aubrey, but we called them Dudu and Nomhamha.

Our beautiful daughter was a complete surprise to both of us, not to mention the nursing staff. Back then, there wasn't the technology of today to tell us that I was carrying two and not one.

When I gave birth to the twins I was relieved that I had resigned rather than taken maternity leave, which would have ended after three or four months. Sol and I decided that I should stay home for a year to look after our little ones, especially since Sol wasn't home most of the time.

I loved that year at home with little Tammie and the twins, watching them all grow and develop, but I missed my job. We also needed the extra salary that I could bring in. After the twins' first birthday, I was ready to go back to work but to my surprise I was pregnant again. I would have to stay home for another year.

By this time I had already started keeping myself busy. I went on a basic dressmaking course at a nearby skills-training place and enjoyed sewing clothes for my children and smart aprons for myself and my mother-in-law. I enrolled to train as a bookkeeper to help me keep proper records of the family funds now that Sol was always away from home. I knew he trusted me, but I wanted to impress him because he was not there to check my calculations any more.

My fourth child, Mongezi, was born on 8 January 1956 at Butterworth. A relative was supposed to accompany us back to East London with the babies, but ended up staying longer with us. That same year, at the end of May, I applied for a job opening at Frere Hospital. The matron was on long leave at the time, so the assistant matron interviewed me instead. I got the job without a problem. My professional career was again on track – or so I thought. But four months later, the matron returned from her long leave and told me to resign so that I could stay home and look after my children. "It's the Christian thing to do," she said.

I was astounded. Why not just come out and tell me I was being fired because I spoke out against unfair treatment? The matron's excuse was hollow – my children were in the excellent hands of my relative while I was at work. It was clear that the so-called Christian government of the day was determined to undermine black professionals. The statement by Dr Hendrik Verwoerd on 17 September 1953 came back to haunt me: "I just want to remind the honourable members that if the native in South Africa today is being taught to expect that he will live his adult life in equality and have equal rights, he is making a big mistake."

I left Frere Hospital that October. Believe me when I say that being marginalised for no reason is very painful. I cheered myself up by holding on to the belief that this was just one failure, a circumstance of my life and not an indication of who I truly was. I chose to be resilient. Fortunately for us, Sol had been promoted to first-grade clerk in charge of the Duncan Village post office in the middle of that year. He no longer had to travel so much for training, and his salary had increased, making it easier for me to stay at home.

That November, I took my children to the baby clinic at the location health centre in Duncan Village for their immunisations and met Sister Dorothy Lubelwana. Dorothy also grew up in Cala and was friends with Olga. She knew I had been forced to leave Frere Hospital. As she helped me with my crying children, she asked me a lot of annoying questions.

"I understand from your sister that you are a strong character," she said. I replied curtly, "Yes, physically I am very strong. I can grind a bag of mielies in a day. Not to say anything about how I can mow down a person with my fist."

The following Friday afternoon, as I peered out, wondering when the rain would stop so that I could dry my washing, someone with a red umbrella walked past the window. I went to the door to ask what the visitor wanted. As the umbrella tilted I saw it was Dorothy.

"My shoes are wet. I will not come in," she said. "I am looking for you, my sister. Please come to work on Monday at 8 am. Come straight to me and make sure you are in your white uniform."

Within a few minutes Dorothy had changed the course of my life. I did not question whether I heard her correctly or not. All I knew was that, come Monday, I would be working again. I was ecstatic. I needed a job to help Sol support our growing family. We both had a burning desire to give them the best care and keep our family together under one roof.

In the pouring rain, I rushed to the public telephones to let Sol know the good news before he left work at 5 pm. He was very happy for me and promised to come home that weekend.

# 9

The Duncan Village health centre, where I now worked, was within walking distance from home and less than a kilometre from the post office. It was also close to the police station and municipal offices. About four kilometres away was the East London central business district. In terms of geography, I could not have asked for a better place to work.

Among the services at the centre was a TB clinic, where Olga worked, and a child health and welfare clinic, where I was placed, working under Sister Ethel Steele. Even though there were no white patients, the centre was mostly managed by white nurses under the authority of a white medical officer.

An important part of my job was doing home visits for immunisations and to gain an understanding of a child's home environment so that we could intervene to ensure that the child developed normally, and to make recommendations on whether or not their parents should receive a government grant or food parcels.

The living conditions of the people in Duncan Village were greatly affected by the Group Areas Act. Duncan Village was regarded as a black blemish in an otherwise white area near the centre of East London. Its proximity made the white people nervous. The state responded by invoking the Group Areas Act, which carved the village up into areas for Indian, coloured and African people. Many Africans were forced to move to a new township called Mdantsane, about twenty-five kilometres away from where they worked. It was common for the people displaced in this way to return to the "African" areas of Duncan Village and put up shacks in any backyard that was available for rent, just to be close to work. This mushrooming of shacks changed the appearance and atmosphere at Duncan Village, causing overcrowding and creating health hazards. Duncan Village went from a location with accessible health facilities, a good school and recreational areas to a virtual squatter camp.

The clinic staff did what they could to improve the community's circumstances. We were fortunate to have the services of social workers, who helped us gather important information about the problems people faced. Armed with this knowledge, we tried to implement appropriate solutions with whatever resources we had.

In 1959, three years after I started working at the clinic, I joined the Young Women's Christian Association – the YWCA – in Duncan Village, through which I became more involved with community work. The YWCA's goal was to uplift society in the face of oppression, to motivate communities to liberate themselves from poor living conditions.

A friend of mine, Nonceba Gush, joined the YWCA at the same time. I first met Mrs Gush in 1957, when she visited the child health clinic with her firstborn child. She was the wife of a teacher who belonged to Sol's dance group, so we had something to talk about from that very first meeting. Mrs Gush was tall and smart, and she had a lovely voice. She was surprised to discover that I already had four children, even though I was only a few years older than her.

My involvement with the YWCA inspired me to improve my own education standards, especially regarding childcare and development. I took a series of short courses, some of them via correspondence, and earned a number of diplomas. I thought that adding to my qualifications would put me in line for promotions at the clinic.

The YWCA ran many interventions to help children, but there was no clear programme to help the aged. In 1962 I took a geriatric care course to improve my understanding of the challenges older people face. I hoped to create a platform for geriatric work through the organisation. By then we were blessed with five children – Tammie, the twins Dudu and Nomhamha, Mongezi, and Andile. My lastborn, Linda, was due in December.

Before long, the YWCA was running a programme for the aged, too. We taught the old people how to knit and sew. The scarves, beanies and aprons they made and sold injected their lives with a sense of purpose. We humans survive spiritually and mentally only if we know that we are making a difference, no matter how small. It was so satisfying to see these old people, who before had worn every one of their years on their faces and bodies, suddenly walk a little more lightly, smile a little more broadly.

The YWCA also served soup to the pensioners on pension-payout days. It was because of this that we were in a position to witness how the municipal police would exploit the old people, unashamedly making them pay for a position near the front of the payout queue. We spoke to liberation leaders like Lawrence Tutu, asking them to intervene. Eventually, a system was put in place whereby pensioners were given numbered cards, so guaranteeing their place in the queue. This prevented the police from interfering and immediately eased tensions. People could stand in long queues without jostling each other.

At Christmas, the YWCA would serve the elderly a magnificent Christmas lunch. We took this opportunity to awaken their minds politically, giving them information that would allow them to form a true picture of what was happening in the country.

I was particularly attached to the elderly programme because I was missing my Mamkhulu and wondering how she was. My visits to her were rather rare at the time. One day in 1963, I paid Mamkhulu a visit to show her my lastborn child, Linda, who was already crawling.

When we arrived, she did not show any interest in the warm slippers I had bought her as a gift, saying they would make her fall. I didn't think anything of it; I thought she just didn't like the slippers. But a short while later she proclaimed joy that her sister's daughter was visiting and had brought her a lovely present. I realised then that old age was attacking her memory, and that she hadn't recognised me at first. It was no surprise. She was, after all, more than eighty years old. I didn't mention my observation to anyone, though. There was no point.

Mamkhulu's two daughters-in-law and a domestic worker were still living with her. They told me that she slept a lot of the time. They speculated that she was lonely. A few months after our visit, I got a call that Mamkhulu had lost her appetite and grown dull and weak with fever. The family had called a doctor, who diagnosed pneumonia, but it was too late. She died in 1964.

Sol and I went to the funeral in Butterworth. Mamkhulu's death left me with a deep feeling of loss. Apart from my mother-in-law, she was the only elderly person that I was close to. It was a consolation that she had witnessed her lessons come to fruition in me, because even though my visits had been scarce in recent years I always wrote to let her know about the changes in my life, about my work and my children, and I enjoyed it when she found the time to reply with her happiness about my progress and efforts.

One of the highlights of my job at the clinic was being allocated a nice, four-roomed house – part of the package for all professionals working for the municipality. This was a big deal. These days, Africans have the option of buying a house. Back then, being given a house was a privilege, not a right. And there was no security of tenure. The house could be taken from you at any time, for no reason other than someone else wanted it and had bribed the township superintendent to get it. Divorced women and widows especially had a hard time of it. The moment a woman's husband died or was out of the picture, she was kicked out.

Our house was semi-detached. Each small room had one small window, and the front and back doors were made of steel. It had a fenced yard with a small garden, and an outside tap next to the toilet. This house was number 711 Bashe Street. There were vegetables from the garden because Sol loved gardening during his spare time.

Our home was a million times better than the wood-and-iron places that people had to endure in other parts of the township. Here twenty families had to share communal water taps and toilets. The most awful thing about these township houses was that they were so overcrowded at times that they constituted a health hazard. As a nurse, it was not pleasant to do rounds to these houses.

Bashe Street was one street away from the library, swimming pool, tennis court, a crèche and a clinic for babies. It was also close to the community hall, which served as a venue for sports activities like boxing and dancing. A music band even practised there. The area was very busy. There were a few shebeens and dagga dealers too.

Raising our children in a highly politicised and socially volatile environment such as Duncan Village between the 1960s and 1980s was a real challenge. Our family's stability was constantly under threat, if not from political intolerance then from the rampant criminal activity that threatened peace and stability in the community.

Sol was worried about raising his children in such an environment and made a point of organising many activities to minimise the destructive influences. As a professional dancer, he already held dance sessions for adults who needed practice. He took this opportunity to involve the youth too. He was also a tennis coach, and encouraged young people to join him whenever he was training children. The parents in the area respected and appreciated his efforts, and encouraged their children to become involved. The Bashe Street area was becoming normal. Even young people from the nearby community benefited from Sol's teachings. The level of delinquency went down as the young people responded to being listened to with respect and interest.

Not all families managed to protect their children from the bad influences of the time. Some Duncan Village families lost the fight. Husbands became abusive, wives grew dissatisfied, children dropped out of school or turned to petty crime. Even in families where both parents were present and responsible, many children became rebellious, usually due to the influence of the type of people they were spending time with. Sol and I took great care to remind our children about their values and to choose their friends wisely.

# 10

Despite the troubled environment in which we lived, our home was full of our happy children, running around everywhere. By 1965, we were blessed with six children – Tammie, the twins Dudu and Nomhamha, Mongezi, and Andile and Linda. I sometimes wondered if they were really all mine, but yes, they were, all six of them.

Tammie, the eldest, was the chatty and confident one. Dudu, the boy twin, was a kind and loving child, if a little tearful and needy of love and care. Even at the age of six, Dudu would ask for help when dressing himself or carrying his bag to school, even though he was fit and healthy enough to carry it himself.

Nomhamha, Dudu's twin, was always neat and particular from an early age. When she was six she refused to stand on the bare floor when she woke up in the morning. She wanted a bedside mat or her slippers. I think she was sometimes lonely, being the only girl among all these brothers. She loved playing with dolls and her younger brothers when they were little, but they soon grew too restless for girls' games and would rather kick a ball around outside. She would then try to help them – and perhaps win them over – by neatly packing all their drawers during the weekends when tidying up her dolls' clothes.

Mongezi, whom we called Tura, performed well at school, especially in the junior years. He was tall and pretended to be Dudu's twin, which amused Dudu at the time. But he was also close to his sister and would help her bake scones for Sol, closely following her instructions. It was almost as though he was a third twin to the two of them.

Andile, our fourth son, was the second perfectionist in the family. Like his father, he was neat, strict and hardworking. From an early age, he liked to be part of a group, whether in doing chores or playing games.

Our lastborn child was Linda, the fifth son of our big family. By the time he was growing up, some of his siblings were at high school already. He was a playful boy and had lots of hand-me-down toys to play with.

In the evenings, during bathtime, the younger ones would splash water all over the floor. Bath time involved more than just plugging a bath and running the water, because of the single outside tap. We had improvised a shower for Sol and me, and for Tammie, who was entering his teens when our youngest was still a toddler. Nomhamha washed in her bedroom with Ntsikie's help. Ntsikie was the trusted nanny Olga had kindly found for my children. For the four youngest boys, Sol and I would move the kitchen table to one side and bring out two zinc bathtubs in the middle of the floor, one bigger than the other. Nine-year-old Dudu and Tura, who was eight, would bath themselves in the one tub while I helped Andile, who was six, and Linda, who was three, in the other.

It sounds like a lot of work, but we were committed to giving our children the best care. Besides, Sol and I both grew up in rural areas, where there was no water on tap. It was easy for us to cobble together a solution. We even got some big metal buckets in which we heated the water on the coal stove.

After the boys had bathed we would wrap them each in a bath towel and they would run into the living room, where their pyjamas would be waiting for them. There they would drop their towels and quickly get dressed, at times pulling on the wrong size by mistake. Dressing time was always a time for laughing because the difference in pyjamas was only in the size and not the colour.

When they were dressed, my heart would melt to see them stand in a straight line, their hands together and eyes tightly closed, ready to say the Lord's Prayer. I was always amused at how they mumbled the words so quickly that you would think they had hot potatoes in their mouths. Afterwards, Sol and I would take out the baths and mop the kitchen floor, teasing each other for having so many children. They were a lot of work and often demanded more energy than we had to give, but we were both grateful to have so much love in our lives. The family is the oldest institution on Earth. I committed to developing my children because they were created inside me and had a role to play in society. I believed – and still believe – that the family is the best structure God has made to raise children to become responsible adults. Sol and I knew, without a doubt, that a happy, stable family would provide a haven of safety and security for our children. I am very pleased to say that we were a happy family.

We became parents in our early and late twenties, so it is true to say that we grew up with our children. We bought books to guide us and consulted with others and each other every step of the way. We believed that if you bring up your children in the right way, they will not deviate from your teachings as adults. So we prioritised love, discipline, support, nurturing and all that goes with it to build the foundations of tolerance, respect, morality and Christianity in our children.

Our children were our friends. We spoke to them and spent time with them. On cold or rainy days, Sol would play indoor games with the children that taught them values such as respect, discipline, honesty and sharing. We encouraged them to ask questions and tried our best to answer them honestly. And we tried to set a good example. Sol and I were very much in love. "I love you" was a common expression in our home. That love rubbed off on our children, who to this day are not scared to express their emotions. Love and honesty develop trust, and I could never attach a value to trust, both giving and receiving it. It was my husband's trust in me that gave me the confidence to grow and be successful, and to learn to trust others. There is no greater tool for personal development.

I would be lying if I said that Sol and I never fought. Once, we got into an argument that ended up involving both our families and a formal traditional apology. It started innocently enough, with a visit from his older sister, Lydia. She enjoyed baking bread and was keen to bake some for us. So she made some dough, put it in a baking tin, revived the fire in the coal stove and shoved the baking tin in, not realising that inside the oven were already bowls of food that I had dished up for the children and left in there to keep warm. It was only later, when she went back to check on the bread, that she saw the smoke of the badly burnt food.

The food had to be thrown away. The children were in tears. Without thinking, I muttered the line that I always used to tease the children with when something went wrong and no one owned up. "Whoever did this should pack their bags and go back to the rural home in Butterworth," I said. The children were scared of the goats and pigs at Sol's family home, so this usually encouraged one of them to own up.

Unfortunately, Lydia took my words to heart. Without us noticing, she packed her small bag and left. It was only when Sol came home that we realised what had happened.

He called his mother at work. He was relieved to find Lydia there. When she told him what I had said, he grew very upset and would not listen to my explanations. The issue became so complicated that I eventually had to go the traditional route of apology, which involved me and two members of my family going to Sol's house in Butterworth that weekend to say sorry to Lydia. I had never seen him so angry.

That Saturday, Uncle Elliot and I left early for Butterworth. Sol went to work. He would join us later, after the post office had closed. Fortunately for me our nanny, Ntsikie, who had witnessed the oven incident, managed to explain to him what I had meant in the time after he finished work but before he could leave for Butterworth. The children confirmed her story. Sol was happy and relieved. He went to Butterworth and explained to his family what had happened, apologising to my family for the trouble caused. It was all over within minutes.

Later on, I wrote Sol a letter to apologise. That was the beginning of a little ritual between the two of us: I would write letters to him to explain myself or raise some issue, and he would read them late at night, after his dancing lessons, over his evening coffee. The letter system worked well, opening long discussions about family issues. In this way our bond grew deeper, along with our ability to trust and support each other.

Sol and I firmly believed our children should help out around the house. Sol drew up a roster, assigning tasks to each child – mostly simple jobs like tidying up the house, washing the dishes and making tea for guests and us when we came home from work – and gave them little financial incentives for effort and jobs well done. In this way, we taught them the importance of taking responsibility and managing their time.

It was amusing to see how different my children were when it came to the chores. Andile, with his love for group work, enjoyed washing dishes with his siblings, and always wanted to be the one to dry the clean dishes before handing them on to someone else to pack away. But the chore he enjoyed the best was polishing the stoep. He loved seeing the stoep gleam in the sunlight after he had polished it. Not so Linda. Many years later, when Andile left to go to boarding school in Standard Six and Linda took over his responsibilities, the job he hated the most was polishing the stoep. We once found him crying on the stoep, complaining that he had hurt his left foot while polishing. But I wasn't convinced because the following morning he complained about his right foot.

While the younger children were still in primary school, Sol and I started a family business on the side, weaving handbags out of sisal and nylon strings. The business was called "Sol-Con Hand Works", a blend of my and Sol's names. Everyone was involved in some way, based on what they enjoyed doing. Sol did the budgeting and placed the orders for materials. Tammie was already at boarding school by then, but when he was around he would help by taking stock of our materials and cutting the string to length. Little Tura would prepare the strings for weaving and hand them on to bigger brother Dudu, who would do most of the weaving, blending the colours of the strings most beautifully. Dudu was the only one of my children who could make a bag from start to finish.

Dudu would then hand the almost-finished bag to me to knit closed, fit the handle and sew in the lining that Nomhamha had made.

Nomhamha was a quick learner – I had only to teach her how to sew the linings once and she never failed to finish her work after that.

Andile would then count and pack the bags if there was an order. During the festive season, he would volunteer to take the bags to the beach to sell to the white tourists. Sol always went with him, to help carry the heavy suitcase filled with bags, and to ensure that they came home safe and sound with the money still in their pockets. I remember Sol telling us one December evening that Andile had refused to leave the beach until he had sold every last one of the handbags in that suitcase. They came home late that day, tired but victorious, carrying a very empty suitcase home.

I worked at the Duncan Village health centre for more than thirty-two years without being promoted, despite being more qualified than many of the white sisters who occupied management positions. These sisters were often dismissive towards me, disregarding the recommendations I made following home visits without understanding the reality of each case.

It is worth noting that, although it was the African nurses who went out on home visits, it was the white nurses who made the final recommendations about who should and should not get state support. None of them so much as set foot in a township home. All they did was read the African nurses' reports.

I once recommended that a family receive financial support because both parents suffered from TB and were not fit for work. However, the sister-in-charge turned down their application because, she said, "They don't look poor." The couple had four children that they would not be able to feed without a grant. Yes, they always looked neat and wore clean clothes. What she didn't notice was that these clothes were always the same.

I had never felt such anger as I felt at that decision. I knew I would do a better job than she did. The injustice of it all provided fertile ground for my political consciousness to grow.

By now I was a full member of the African National Congress (ANC). My home was often used as a place for people to come and refresh themselves on the way to political rallies held at the community hall just around the corner. Many important political meetings were held at that hall.

Not all the white sisters were so blinkered, of course. The sister in charge of my clinic, Sister Ethel Steele, was a pillar of strength and kindness to all. She made it her business to understand what life in the townships was like, and formed a powerful link between white charities and the people of Duncan Village. During the forced removal of families from Duncan Village to Mdantsane in the sixties, it was Sister Steele who organised a mobile clinic to reach mothers that had been relocated far from our clinic. She arranged for companies that sell baby food to donate samples and dented tins to our clinic, and also arranged a vegetable market in Duncan Village so that people wouldn't have to pay for transport just to buy a few groceries.

We were very sad indeed when Sister Steele told us she was going home to England. Whether she was leaving to escape the Special Branch or whether she was emotionally and physically burnt out from working with East London's poorest, most neglected communities, I will never know. One thing I do know is that white liberals were made to pay for acknowledging the humanity of the African person. People like Sister Steele were despised by the state, terrorised by the Special Branch and called derogatory terms like *kaffirboetie* – brother to *kaffirs*.

The Special Branch seemed to be everywhere in those days. They believed that the YWCA – because of its principles of justice and freedom for all – was a "disruptive" influence on the children it worked with. They severely harassed the youth and caused great turmoil in the community. Many children had no choice but to abandon their education and go into exile to join the liberation forces. In most cases, parents didn't know whether their children had fled the country or been taken by the Special Branch. Both generations suffered incredibly.

There was not much the YWCA could do for the Duncan Village community beyond help its people develop a sense of self-esteem and leadership. It organised youth activities such as concerts, drama competitions and drum majorettes, and put together a scheme where young ones could do paid work for an hour a day during the school holidays. This scheme earned them some money to boost their confidence and help their households. It ran a soup kitchen for pensioners and, together with my clinic, started day-care centres for the elderly.

In time, I became involved with the YWCA at a regional level. Because of East London's proximity to rural Ciskei and Transkei, the association helped train many rural women in agriculture. The migrant labour laws resulted in men leaving their families behind in the Transkei while they went to the cities in search of work. Many women were left behind in poverty, helplessly waiting for their husbands to send back what little money they were able (and willing) to spare.

The YWCA offered these women courses in animal husbandry, piggery and poultry farming as a way to improve their income and living conditions. The traditional leaders supported the initiative, giving us permission to visit and make use of the land. Working closely with the United Democratic Front, the Council of Churches and youth movements, we also ran projects that taught these women self-help skills, sewing, beadwork and even food production.

In 1980, I took over presidency of the Albany Border and Ciskei YWCA. By this time my friend Mrs Gush was the General Secretary for the area. We worked together well as a team, and often travelled to national YWCA committee meetings.

YWCA members from all over the country were often given the opportunity to travel to other parts of the world to deliver essential items, study or learn about what other women were doing and to develop the skills of rural women. Mrs Gush once visited a YWCA in Kenya, where she learnt how to make mud stoves, cement water-tanks and toilets for toddlers.

One of the first things I did when I took over as the regional president was start a programme to deliver essential items like sanitary pads, soap and wound dressings to young people, especially women, in exile at a camp in Namibia. Mrs Gush and I once travelled there together.

Between 1978 and 1983, I also travelled to Lesotho quite often, sometimes on YWCA business and sometimes to attend political rallies. Dudu had a car by then. On a few occasions he took Andile and myself to Lesotho to listen to Chris Hani and Alfred Pat Nzo speak. The event organisers usually helped pay for attendees' petrol. On such trips we usually took along toiletries and jerseys for the

1950
*Sol in his ballroom dancing suit ready to take to the floor.*

1950
*At Coronation Hospital: Second-year student nurses about to leave. I am on the far right.*

1950 →
Attending a function at
the local community hall.

↑
1950
Uncle Elliot Silwana, a
pillar of strength for me
during times of need.

January 1957

We occupied this Duncan Village home for more than 30 years. One of our sons st.
uses the home today. We intend to preserve it as a place where we treasure and
secure family memories to assist future generations to know where they come fro.

1961

At a Duncan Village get together. I am second from the left. The others, left to
right are Nombeko Mjindi, Ms Qunta, and Ivy Mbobo.

1962
Professional nurses enjoying themselves. I am at the
front right.

...CA ladies donated blankets to this old age home. I am seated on the left and my
...Olga Dangazele is second from the right in the back row.

1962

1964
Nomhamha (far right) at her birthday with her friends.

1966
Linda on his fourth birthday, with his cousins, Ntuntu on his right and Sbongile on his left in the front. At the back from the left are Tura, Andile (with hand up), Nomhamha (in front) and Dudu.

1966

At a farewell function for graduating midwives at Frere Hospital hall, with the band at the back. I am seated second from the right, with Vuyiswa's hands on my shoulders.

1975

Watching my YWCA youth drum majorettes' performance passing my house in Duncan Village.

1975
Sol and I entering the
community centre hall at
Duncan Village for a function

1982
YWCA ladies at a conference at Peddie welcomed Mrs Rampomane, a visiting member
from Soweto. I am in a red dress behind the lady on the far right.

1986 ↻

*Sol speaking at his farewell function at the post office.*

1988

*Tammie and his wife during their wedding anniversary at our Butterworth home.*

1988
At Tammie's wedding anniversary (left to righ_ is Sdumo (my half broth me, Tammie and his wife (my brother), Olga (my s Nozie Lavisa, and Sol. is kneeling in the front.

1994
Family friends wait_ vote for the first ti_ their lives. My siste_ is second from the _ a scarf on her head_ Dorothy Lubelwana the far right.

1996
A proud father: Sol and his son Andile at a graduation ceremony at Wits.

2004
Tura at Nomhamha
and Dudu's 50th
birthday party.

2005
Linda and his sister, Nomhamha, enjoying
themselves at Karland near Tsitsikamma in
the Eastern Cape.

2005
My grandsons at a traditional occasion.

2005
My grandsons at a family wedding.

2005
Andile and Svieta celebrate their wedding traditionally.

2006
At my grandson Kanya's welcome home
celebrations from his initiation ceremony.
Granddaughters enjoying themselves.

2006
...omhamha amongst the
...en enjoying Kanya's
ceremony.

2007
A photo of the young
Sol and me displayed
by our proud children
at our fifty-seventh
wedding anniversary
celebration. Below: a
special invitation card.

You are cordially invited
to the

57th Wedding Anniversary

of

*Silumko* & *Manise*
Ngcaba

Date: Saturday, 22 December 2007
Time: 11am
Venue: East London City Hall

R.S.V.P. to 082 210 3690 or 043 741 1998

2007
Sol and I attending a
Mqanduli Anglican Church
service.

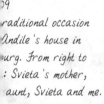

09
raditional occasion
Andile's house in
urg. From right to
: Svieta's mother,
aunt, Svieta and me.

2010
Speaking at Sivu's
twenty-first birthday.

2011
At Laugh & Learn Educare, at the end of every year, the six-year-olds graduate and their send off is always blessed by the presence of all the parents. Standing is Svieta Ngcaba one of the Trustees of the Centre.

2010
Dudu and Siyabulela at Sivu's twenty-first birthday.

2011
Nomhamha's farewell function at Cecilia Makiwane Hospital with her father on her left. To her right is her cousin, Mrs Mpumie Tshisela née Silwana, and her close friend Mrs Nambitha Metuse. The three of them practised as professional nurses for many years.

2012

Family photo during the twins' birthday. Seated from left are Linda
Lavisa, myself, Sol, Nomhamha (twin) and Svieta. Behind us stand
Dudu (twin), Linda and Andile.

2012

Sol is relaxing. He is eighty-eight years old.

young exiles. A few times we even delivered education certificates to exiles from their families in Duncan Village so that they could apply to study further elsewhere. That was how things worked back then: we helped each other out.

The special branches of both South Africa and the homelands always took the opportunity to harass people coming home from such trips. Their women officers searched me at East London airport, looking for ANC documents that they thought I was bringing in to distribute. Of course, they were never lucky enough to find anything. We were not stupid enough to expose ourselves like this, when the trains were full of mine workers carrying banned literature in their big trunks as they crossed the country.

While the YWCA was never affiliated to any political party, it did provide a platform for political thought. I am proud to say that I was among those who spoke out and wanted to be heard. I believe that the strength of being a mother gave me – and others like me – the power to care, love and protect all human beings to the best of my ability.

Some parents became suspicious about the YWCA. They thought that we were recruiting their children to leave the country. We did not know much about Umkhonto we Sizwe then, but we had a common fear of the killings and the disappearance of our children. It made me sad, this sense of distrust, when everything we did was for the sake of all African people. Perhaps the Special Branch played a part in breaking down the confidence the community had in us.

By 1980, my children were young adults themselves. They had completed their schooling at rural boarding schools because it seemed to Sol and me that "broken" families were more common in urban areas. Tammie had studied business management and was working at Albany Bakeries, and Nomhamha was a professional nurse at Cecilia Makiwane Hospital in Mdantsane.

Dudu was a teacher at Ikhwezi Higher Primary in Duncan Village and was very politically active. He had been arrested a number of times. In 1981 he was arrested on suspicion of bringing banned literature into the country from Lesotho and other areas. He was in prison over the first birthday of his firstborn son, so the celebration had to be postponed. The state could never prove it, though, and he was freed in the end.

Tura had started studying a Bachelor of Commerce at Fort Hare University but dropped out after being detained a number of times. He was the chairperson of the Duncan Village Youth Movement, which was a prominent player in the struggle in our area. He had been arrested in 1978 for distributing banned literature. He waited in jail for ten months before his case finally appeared before the court and he was proved innocent. Soon after his release, he was charged with inciting students to join the ANC at Blythswood High in 1964. The case was thrown out of court when the judge found out that Tura was only six years old at the time.

Andile had been arrested and detained on suspicion of building bombs and had been very badly treated by the Special Branch.

Every time one of my sons was arrested for their political involvement, I felt a terrible blend of fear for their safety and pride in their courage and sense of justice. I thought about them every day and prayed for their safe return. Fortunately, for those of us who were part of the struggle, the belief that freedom in South Africa could be a reality in our lifetimes made us strong.

At about this time Dudu, Tura and I became involved with forming the Duncan Village Residents' Association and its branches. The association was to be part of the United Democratic Front, a coalition of civic, students' and workers' organisations.

Early in 1981, at the age of twenty-three, Andile went into exile. Not once did he give me any hint that he had been thinking about leaving the country. Young men were so committed to secrecy about the ANC in those days. I only found out about it when we were advised by our contacts in Lesotho that he had gone there and wasn't coming home again. He was waiting for safe passage out of the country.

I was devastated that he hadn't told us his plans, but relieved that he would be out of harm's way. Nomhamha visited Lesotho to take him some of his belongings. He left the country soon after.

# 12

In 1981, under the auspices of the YWCA, Mrs Gush and I visited Ntabethemba, near Whittlesea. Ntabethemba was a refugee camp, the direct result of the apartheid government forming Ciskei as a new "independent" homeland just south of Transkei, which had been independent since 1976. Many families left Transkei and moved to Ciskei – whether in search of a better life or because they were fearful of what would happen if they stayed, I don't know – where they were forced to live in a refugee camp. The camp was in a sandy area, making it difficult to secure tents to the ground, except for the corners. There was no privacy. Anyone passing could easily see the legs of family members as they sat inside the tent. It made my heart ache. It seemed particularly cruel to me that they named the refugee camp "Ntabethemba", which means "Hill of Hope".

After taking stock of what people needed most, Mrs Gush and I returned to East London to stock up. We gathered toys and books for the children and warm clothing for the elderly. When we left East London to return to the camp, we co-opted two white women who were visiting the YWCA to come with us. When we arrived at the camp, we noticed some police vans parked at the entrance that hadn't been there before. We stopped the car.

A man in uniform knocked on the window. "Permits," he said in Xhosa.

Mrs Gush and I looked at each other. "We were just here this morning."

"You still need permits."

"We don't have any. We're with the YWCA on charity work."

The policeman's eyebrows furrowed. "Come. Out the car." He pointed at our two passengers. "You too. Out. You're trespassing. We're taking you to the police station." By now his colleagues had joined him.

"Our car is full of things for the refugees. We're not leaving it here," said Mrs Gush. "We will follow you to the police station."

The policemen conferred with each other, then reluctantly agreed. We followed them to the Mdantsane police station. "What is happening? Where are we going?" asked one of our passengers.

I explained the situation as best I could. I did not add that I suspected that it was their presence that had attracted the police's attention. In those days, it was unusual – and virtually an offence in itself – to see African and white people sitting side by side.

When we arrived at Mdantsane police station, we were each given a pile of forms to fill in our personal information. By now it was early evening. Mrs Gush and I were channelled into a small office with two comfortable armchairs and given two big, clean towels. We could hear someone, perhaps one of our visitors, speaking English next door.

We waited. No one came to speak to us, or give us food or water. After a long time, the door opened. A woman stood there with a surprised look on her face. "Are you still here?" she said. Then she stepped aside. "You can go."

Mrs Gush and I walked out of the police station and went to the car, where we were soon joined by the two white women. I looked at my watch. It was 6 am. We had not been charged, since we had not broken any laws. We were just being harassed, pure and simple. I was embarrassed to have subjected our visitors to such a situation, but I also knew the experience would give them insight into what was happening in the country, and a story to talk about.

This was just an example of how the security police would use any excuse to harass people. Our night in jail was only harassment, but they thought nothing of murdering those who fought for freedom simply to ensure that they got their monthly salaries and were promoted for being cruel. I still cannot understand how young men who were once so close to the African nannies and gardeners who looked after them when they were little could grow to become so determined to hate and oppress. It says something about what their own families taught them, I think.

After we were released, we went home to clean up and rest, and made our way to the refugee camp again – without our white visitors, this time. When we handed out the clothes, toys and books, one of the camp residents said to us, "We are grateful to Sebe for sending us these donations."

I was astounded. The man thought that the donations we brought had come from Lennox Sebe, Ciskei's president. The reality was that Sebe was a pawn of the apartheid government, a compliant puppet installed to "rule" the homeland. He didn't care about his people, and the country he ruled was a sham, created by the apartheid government to create the perception of independence when really it was just another way to enforce apartheid on their terms.

His comment made me realise just how much people believed in the homeland system, and how much work lay ahead of us. We had to combat the apartheid government's divide-and-rule tactics. Xhosas here, Zulus there, Sotho-speaking people there – homelands for all. This policy of separation had to be destroyed.

When we got home, the security forces continued their harassment. It wasn't as though they were picking on us in particular – they persecuted most people. They would visit us at work, at home, day and night, trying their best to make us worry as they fished for information or anything that could be of benefit to them. Once, during one of their usual unannounced visits, a half-full pot of cooked samp and beans secured our passports' safety from their grubby hands.

My involvement in our country's struggle for freedom was always a very personal one. I didn't get tangled up in the political hierarchy and theoretical debates. All I did was speak up when I thought someone had to, and step in when I thought that something had to be done. So it should not come as a surprise that I opened my house to young men fleeing to exile. It was my way of healing the empty feeling of my missing son, of realising my hopes that someone had fed him and offered him a place to rest as he made his way to join those who were fighting more actively for our freedom.

One night about a year after Andile's disappearance, only half an hour after six young men had left my house on their way to Lesotho, there was a loud knocking at my door. I opened the door and members of the Special Branch poured in, searching the house for the young fugitives. Of course, they were too late. Their search was futile. They were just about to give up when one of the African policemen spotted a dirty dish with six spoons in the kitchen.

My insides turned to jelly. I had cooked the young men a platter of mince and rice before they left, giving them each a spoon with which to eat. They left after midnight and I went to bed without washing the dirty dishes that now told tales in my kitchen. The African policeman pointed at the spoons and shouted, "Where are these people? Tell us now!"

His colleagues all rushed to witness his discovery and even counted the spoons, again and again. They started getting angry and abusive. They promised to arrest me if I did not tell them the truth. "Tshini!" I said, thinking quickly. "Leave me alone! I was only feeding my tokoloshes."

"My God!" screamed one of them, jumping to the door. "We should go! This woman is a witch!"

They left and I went safely back to bed. Superstition has its uses, I realised, especially for those who believe in it.

# 13

By 1985, political activity throughout the country was increasing. The Duncan Village Residents' Association, which my sons and I had started working towards five years before, was finally launched a month before the first state of emergency was declared in July 1985.

We found out that the state was planning to forcibly remove even more families to Mdantsane. Many residents still remembered the trauma of the removals in the sixties, and decided to resist the move. Dudu and I were involved with calling on the Peace and Justice Commission, the legal fraternity and the Border Council of Churches to help us fight against the move. The struggle was getting stronger. Duncan Village was becoming very tense. Activists were constantly being harassed, many were arrested. Black-on-black violence increased, the result of mistrust planted in people's minds by the Special Branch, which seemed to think that the United Democratic Front, the YWCA and the ANC were one and the same.

On 11 August 1985, Victoria Mxenge, a Durban-based civil rights lawyer, was assassinated and buried at nearby Rayi village. She was a defender of the struggle, helping to protect young activists who had been detained from torture and death. After her funeral, returning mourners set fire to some government and school buildings. It was as though those fires spread to the hearts and minds of the young people in Duncan Village, and by the following morning, Duncan Village was ablaze. Groups of young people had gone around the village, burning down the homes and cars of community councillors, policemen and members of the community suspected of working with the Special Branch. The state responded by sending in the police and the army. They brought the uprising to a bloody end, killing at least thirty-one people.

The state dropped the idea of relocating Duncan Village to Mdantsane after the massacre, but I didn't feel as though we had won any victory. The murder of those young activists made me redouble my efforts to oppose the unjust system that we were being subjected to. In the months that followed, the YWCA became more involved with organising programmes to increase awareness against oppression. These included a two-day conference at Debe Nek Bible School in Ciskei starting on 16 June 1986, the tenth anniversary of the Soweto uprising.

A few days before the conference, it was my turn for the police to come knocking on my door. I kept quiet for a while, listening. I was alone in the house. Sol was living near King William's Town, close to his work in Bisho, and only came home weekends. Tura and Linda were asleep in the back room and wouldn't hear the noise. The banging was insistent, as though the person was being chased by a lion and needed protection. After a good few minutes, I gathered up my courage and went to the door.

"Who is it?" I called.

Mens' voices answered me, deep and in unison, a choir of devilish spirits. "Amapolisa! Vula Mama! It's the police, Mama. Open up!"

I opened the door. A handful of Special Branch members rushed in, shouting insults as they usually did. *Again, this harassment!* I thought. I became very calm, expecting them to search my house, throw everything upside down and then leave. Such experiences were common, especially in families with young adults. But they just came in and stood around in the lounge. I knew then that this was a different type of a visit. Normally, they would scatter into the house, asking questions about family members, swearing and calling them names. I never bothered answering, because there really were no answers for them.

Two of them came up close to me. One of them said, "Be quick! Dress. We want you. Don't run away." The way he spoke made me think I was suspected of robbing a bank. Can you imagine?

I was about to argue when a colleague of theirs came closer. Perhaps he thought I would be scared of him because he was white. I recognised him. He had been watching our house almost daily for months. "Madam, please dress and come with us," he said.

I walked into my bedroom. It felt as though they had been in my house for hours already. Bees hummed in my head. I was utterly confused. I would pick up a jersey, transfer it to my other hand and put it down. I would choose something else, hold it for a few minutes and again put it down before returning to the jersey, backwards and forwards, not really knowing what I was doing.

When they eventually led me out the front door I was greeted by a scene I shall never forget. There were four different types of vehicle lined up at the front gate. Imagine: four police cars, filled with policemen, all coming to fetch one fifty-seven year-old woman! It was absurd. Then I looked down the street and realised that I was not the only one being arrested. More groups of people were being led out of their homes and taken to the police vans, among them Dudu, who lived two streets away.

Dudu saw that they were taking me too and said to one of the policemen. "Guys, can't you allow my mother to get something warmer? It's very cold." He was right. I had not realised how cold it was. They ushered me back into the house. I closed my bedroom door and dressed warmly. I then tucked a small towel and a small warm shawl under my arm, not realising at that time how handy these two items would be.

I was marched to a big yellow van that was too high for me to climb into without help. Inside, the smell of tobacco and dirty feet choked me. The van soon filled up and started moving, going so quickly that I had to hold on to the bars.

At Fleet Street police station, two policemen helped me out of the van. I had been at the police station for half an hour when the state of emergency was extended to cover the whole country at midnight on 12 June 1986. There was a lot of movement and excitement among the uniformed staff. I couldn't understand their reaction. I was worried about being away from home and wondered why I had been detained. I didn't consider what the state of emergency might mean for me. A little later, a policeman fetched me and took me to a very small cell with a cement floor. It had a dim light, a toilet in the corner and a cement bunk. He threw damp blankets at my feet and banged the door closed behind him.

The blankets reeked of urine, and a vile smell quickly filled the room, suffocating me. I covered my head and face with my shawl but could only tolerate that for a few minutes. I could not breathe properly. I closed my eyes, telling myself it all would be over soon. By now the walls and ceilings appeared to be moving inwards, as if to crush me. That was terribly frightening for me.

I cried bitterly. Eventually the tears started to ease up and I started to console myself that this was the price we had to be prepared to pay if we were ever going to be free. I reminded myself of the many people I knew who had been detained and survived – my sons among them. I told myself this was an experience that would strengthen me. I prayed that God would give me understanding and tolerance. That gave me relief. I allowed myself to accept the situation.

Later, much later, I opened my eyes and saw light coming in under the door. It was the day after the longest night of my life. I heard a key opening the door. As I walked towards it, hope filled my heart. I could hear freedom songs. I couldn't see anybody, but the voices were clear. Somewhere, people were singing.

I was allowed to drink water from a tap with a mug chained to it. Later, I joined seven other women standing in line to have their fingerprints taken. We were all very happy to see each other. Though we did not know each other, we felt a common bond. Captives as we were, we were like sisters. They told me that close to 200 men had been arrested that night in Duncan Village alone. I found out later that, in addition to Dudu, my sons Tura and Linda had also been detained, although Linda was released almost immediately as he was not on the Special Branch's list.

After the fingerprinting process we were transferred to Fort Glamorgan prison in East London. Everything was quiet there, and it looked clean. The buildings had very high walls. A few uniformed guards patrolled the rooftops with their rifles, ready to shoot. A number of uniformed women, both black and white, sat behind a long counter in the admissions office. The clock on the wall showed 11 am when we arrived.

I felt tired as I waited for my turn to be admitted, so I leant against the wall. "Prisoner, that wall is not falling," snapped one of the African warders. "Move away from it."

I laughed and said, "I'm sorry, but my name is Connie Ngcaba. Mrs."

This elicited laughter from one of the other warders. "Mrs," she said, her tone mocking. "We shall see, Mrs."

Our valuables were taken from us and locked away. We were searched and told to take off all our clothes. Still naked, we were told to jump, as though that would dislodge something that might have been concealed somewhere. I had never known such humiliation.

After a shower, we were examined by a young woman doctor. She introduced herself as Dr Botha. I asked her whether she was related to Pik Botha, the Minister of Foreign Affairs. She said she didn't know him and her father wasn't a politician. She spoke to us kindly about detention and the state of emergency. We responded positively to her, despite the degradation we had suffered at the hands of her colleagues.

Our final destination was a big prison cell with a pile of blankets at the entrance. Two woman warders were there to supervise us. We were told to each take two blankets, a thin sponge mattress to sleep on and a towel. As I moved back so that I should be served last, I saw dust fly as each blanket was opened and checked for holes and lice. Within minutes the room was full of dust. My eyes itched and my nose ran. I began to sneeze, again and again. I went to stand next to a very narrow window but the opening was too small, it did not give me enough fresh air. My face started swelling up. My fellow prisoners begged that I be allowed out, but the warders were reluctant.

The brave detainees then took matters into their own hands. They started shouting loudly, clapping hands and whistling. Within a few minutes a nurse, a social worker and two other warders came rushing in. Seeing my distress they led us all to a small hall where the air was clean and I could breathe again. This was to be our cell for the next two months. We were given new blankets, sponge mattresses and towels. I told them I was a nurse and asked for an antihistamine, which they gave me. A small victory, given what was to come.

# 14

If there is ever a time when I feel the need to be alone, to escape the mad rush of urban living, a South African prison is the last place I would choose to visit.

After four weeks in detention, the interrogations started. The Special Branch headquarters was at Cambridge Police Station, in one of the suburbs of East London. Detainees were picked up from the prison for three or four hours of interrogation every day. Some prisoners were taken once a month, some once every two weeks, some only now and then. I was one of those they fetched every week.

The interrogations at Cambridge were very frightening. Many people were physically tortured, although thankfully I was not one of them.

Every time I went I was questioned by a different interrogator. I would be asked the same questions again and again. It seemed to me that they were trying to learn the names of the struggle leaders and organisers. To me, no single person could be responsible for creating an uprising. An uprising was caused by the oppression of masses. Each time I answered them openly, hoping that they would finally leave me alone, but each time they kept coming back with the same questions. It was humiliating and disempowering – a psychological game for them. The part I found the most mortifying was how meals were handled while I waited in a cell to be taken to the interrogation room: they would throw a plate of food in under the door and let it slide towards me, as though I was a dog. I would not wish that kind of treatment on my worst enemy.

Our families did not know where we were being kept for the first eight weeks of detention. Sol and Nomhamha checked all the East London police stations looking for me and my sons. Linda had been released on the night he was detained because his name was not on the security police's list, but he immediately fled to the Transkei. Tura and Dudu were still in detention, in the men's section of Fort Glamorgan.

Those first eight weeks were traumatic for Sol and my daughter. They were scared for us. A lot was happening in those days. Eventually they were told where we were being held. They had to sign forms with visitation rules before they could see us. We were only allowed one visitor per week. They were not allowed to give us food or clothes during visits.

One afternoon a warder summoned me to the front. "You have a visitor," she said, and marched me into a very small office with a chair and a counter topped with a wall of glass. There were a few holes through the glass at face level. Someone walked in the door on the other side of the glass partition. It was Sol. We looked at one another.

"You have twenty minutes," said the warder, making herself comfortable on the only chair in the room.

It upset me to see how much weight Sol had lost. It was shocking to see a free man, who slept on his own bed and ate his own food in his own house, look so thin. Like a ghost with glassy eyes. A tear ran down one cheek. His lips trembled.

I realised that I, too, looked terrible. I had lost a lot of weight and the skin on my face was dry and rough. I realised I had to do something to prevent him from going into shock. I lifted my hand, putting my palm flat on the glass. "Hello, Mr Beginner," I said. "May I have this dance?"

Sol raised his hand to mine and he smiled. "Manse, I am glad you are alive. This will all be over one day, my dear. Don't worry."

By now I had to hold back my own tears. I managed to tell him the boys were in the men's section.

"Did you see them? How did they look?"

I didn't want to tell him that I hadn't seen them. "We'll all be home soon," I said, trying to reassure him.

We were quiet for some minutes, just staring at each other. He seemed honestly relieved to see me alive. In those days, loved ones sometimes disappeared forever. There was nothing left to say to each other. All we could do was push our palms against the glass, wishing it would break.

The warder stood and started leading me away. I turned to go. Behind me, I heard Sol's voice. "I will always love you. No matter where you are," he said. I was out the door before he finished his sentence so I couldn't reply, although I could feel in that moment that we shared the pain of separation anew.

Sol's visit haunted me for days. I kept thinking of all the things that I should have said, but didn't. I was also torn with guilt for what I had done to my family. Seeing my husband look so neglected made me realise that my family was suffering because of my political activities.

Then I thought about my dear mother. She had been a dedicated domestic servant for the Robertson family for many years, although her poor living conditions next door to them did not portray the respect they claimed to have for her when talking about her good service to the congregation at her funeral. I'm certain they meant well, but they failed to follow up their words with action. It occurred to me that my political involvement, as painful as it was for Sol and my children now, was my way of trying to improve their lives in future.

The following week it was my daughter's turn to visit me. Nomhamha said a lot of comforting words about her father. She said he was visiting my sons and would visit me again the following week. She made sure she planted good memories in my mind.

She noticed that my head was covered in a crust of very itchy sores. She managed to arrange a special permit for Dr Olivia Bikitsha to see me. Dr Bikitsha practised in East London but was originally from Butterworth and would, we knew, give me good treatment. After suffering for so many weeks, what was worse was the problem of washing my itchy head twice a day because each cell had only one shower.

The week after that, Sol visited again. This time we had a lot to say to each other, and spoke to each other lovingly. We even managed to share a sense of acceptance for our situation, which was completely beyond our control.

Even so, being degraded, seeing my husband suffer so and being deprived of basic sanitation made me formidably resentful. I felt my mind growing distracted by hate. The following week, on Nomhamha's second visit, she tried to cheer me up by telling me how my precious grandchildren were doing. To the dismay of us both, we realised I had forgotten their names. Nomhamha was hurt and worried. She feared that I was so depressed that I might lose my mind.

During the third month we were transferred out of the hall and back to a large prison cell, where I joined forty other women who had been detained from all over East London and Mdantsane. The cell had high cement walls and was about six metres wide and twenty metres long. A series of narrow windows ran down the long walls. At night, we hung our clothes out of these windows to dry.

There was no furniture. At night we slept on our thin mattresses and during the day we rolled them up, neatly placed our folded blankets on top and sat on them. The only noteworthy features were a small bathroom with thin walls housing two toilets and a single shower, and the door in the corner – the only way in and out.

The cell was crowded but what the warders didn't realise was that this togetherness created the perfect opportunity to motivate each other and pass on news about the Struggle. We told others about the United Democratic Movement being formed, and took the opportunity to tell others about the rent boycott and our rights as detainees. Prison turned into a venue for illegal political workshops.

Other than that, our days were characterised by grinding monotony. We would wake up at 4 am, not because we had to, but because it was the only way we all got the chance to shower in the single cubicle, even though we washed two at a time. After everyone was clean and dressed, we lined up in the middle of the room for a head count, after which we marched in pairs down a long passage to the dining hall for breakfast at 7 am, our hands behind our backs.

The dining hall was large and drafty, the cold amplified by the fact that the tables, mugs and plates were all metal. Breakfast consisted of very hot black coffee and porridge without sugar. Lunch was served at 11.30 am and consisted of plain samp and either soya soup or mince. We ate dinner early, at 4 pm. It consisted of black coffee again, with very cold bread and drippings for spread. The meals changed a little here and there, but by and large this is what we ate.

There were four cells in our wing of the prison, each positioned in such a way as to form a square of lawn in the middle. We were allowed to walk around on these lawns about twice a week, if the weather allowed it. It was always such a relief to see the sky, and feel the sun on my skin.

One benefit of these trips to the Special Branch headquarters in Cambridge was that we were allowed to visit the small library and tuck shop in the corner of the prison once a week. There were Bibles to read in each cell, but being able to take out one different book each week provided me with a thin anchor to sanity.

During the first week of April 1987, I was punished for reading a book in the light from the passage after lights out. I was sent to solitary confinement for fourteen days. I was taken to a cell the size of a door with a toilet against the wall and a single window that was open all the time. I had no contact with people. My meals were shoved in under the door – a favourite method of humiliation, apparently.

I am someone who gets enjoyment from contact with other people, my family especially. Solitary confinement was torture to me. I felt disoriented. Within days a pervasive sense of helplessness pierced my heart. I started talking to myself, just to hear the sound of a human voice. I spoke about my thirty years' experience in child health care with the tiles on the wall. I started feeling stronger, more purposeful.

Then I heard a voice. Someone was listening and responding. Someone wanted to know more. By the time the warders eventually took me back to the cell, instead of feeling cowed, I felt a renewed sense of energy and resolve. Given everything that was being done to African people, two weeks of suffering was a comparatively short time.

April 19 was my birthday. The Special Branch fetched me as usual, but on this day there was no questioning. I was allowed to look at my birthday cards from my family, my colleagues, some neighbours and my dear friend, Mrs Gush, signed by herself and a few YWCA members. I also received a few cards from the national YWCA office in Johannesburg. These were signed by Joyce and Rachel Seroke, the YWCA's secretary-generals at the time, and other well-known women activists. There was even a card from the international YWCA office in Switzerland signed by Phumzile Mlambo-Ngcuka and others. The Special Branch seemed surprised to find that my imprisonment was known beyond our borders. The solidarity I felt on that day made me so proud of being a member of the YWCA.

They started releasing detainees from our cell in May 1987. My turn came in June. Two warders came to the cell door after lunch and called out two names. My heart started beating fast when I heard that mine was one of them.

"Collect your things and come to the door."

Those sweet words changed my life. I tried to contain my excitement because with the laws of our country back then you never knew what was coming next.

"You're number nineteen and twenty," someone announced.

We gathered our meagre belongings and were ushered to the front office, where we signed for our valuables. I was given my belongings and birthday cards in a plastic bag. The Special Branch picked us up, took us to the nearest taxi rank and gave us R5 to find our own way home.

I decided to put in one last foot of resistance, refusing to get out of the combi. "You men had better drop me off at home," I shouted. "Take me back where you found me!"

"We're not allowed to do that," said one policeman.

"Number 711 Bashe Street, Duncan Village," I said, making it clear that I would not move.

Eventually they dropped me off at the front gate of my house. I had lost so much weight the neighbours did not recognise me at first. It was 9 June 1987. After a year in detention, I finally slept on my own bed in my own house. It was like a dream come true.

# 15

My time in detention cost Sol his job. After thirty-six years of working for the government in the post office, he was forced to retire immediately because members of his family were suspected of being ANC activists.

I was to endure a similar form of dismissal. I returned to work a month after my release, in July 1987. In no time I was told that I had to retire in two years' time, when I turned sixty. There was nothing I could do. Even though we had bought a house in Gompo township the year before, I retired in April 1989. Fortunately, by this time Sol had found a job as a bookkeeper for a supermarket. Between his salary and pension, we managed to pay for the house and our living costs.

My sons Tura and Dudu were released a year after I was freed. In all, they had spent two years in detention, also undergoing regular interrogations and even torture. One of the questions the police kept asking Dudu was why they allowed their home to be a people's home. I don't think there is any answer to a question like that.

My family was one of many that contributed to the Struggle. We did not regret our political involvement. It was our moral duty, our responsibility and our right. We were not surprised that the security forces did not spare us. We were, after all, enemies of the state. The official stance was that they were "protecting the rule of the law". *From whom?* I always wondered.

At this time, more and more young people were fleeing the country, going into exile rather than risk being detained, tortured or shot just for of the colour of their skin. Andile was still out of the country. We hadn't heard from him in nearly eight years when, in 1989, two years after my release from detention, we got a telephone call at our Gompo home.

"I have a message from Andile," said the person on the other side. "He will be in Lusaka in December. It would make him very happy if you could meet him there."

My heart beat loudly in my ears and my legs almost gave in under me. Until then, I didn't even know that my son was alive. I called a family meeting and we decided that Dudu and I would go.

We applied for passports. Through the actions of some impimpi – a snitch – the security forces learned about our preparations and they did their best to prevent us from getting our passports. Fortunately for us, there were people in the Home Affairs office who were sympathetic to the struggle and gave the wrong information about our itinerary.

We finally received our passports less than a week before we were due to leave on 20 December 1989. We took an early flight from East London to Johannesburg, from where we took a connecting flight to Gaborone in Botswana and then on to Lusaka Airport in Zambia.

We arrived in Lusaka at about 8 pm. Dudu and I were not the only family members travelling to visit their long-lost exiled loved ones, and as we disembarked, we heard freedom songs being sung by a group in the distance. We moved closer to the sound and I saw someone running towards us. When I saw it was Andile I lost control of myself and cried out, "Umntwanam! Umntwanam! My child! My child!"

We hugged each other, tears were rolling down my cheeks and my heart full of unbelievable joy after missing him for so many years. Then my sons embraced, and my heart almost broke with the joy of seeing my sons cling to each other.

I looked around at the other members of the group. I knew some of them, and recognised many others. Andile, a few of his comrades, Dudu and I climbed into a combi and were taken to the hotel where they were staying. Dudu and I couldn't stop asking questions. We learnt that Andile had been an Umkhonto we Sizwe commander in Angola. I was so grateful that he had survived that war.

We spent eighteen wonderful days with Andile, talking, catching up, going to ANC meetings with him and his comrades. We even attended the ANC's anniversary celebrations on 8 January. Dudu and I were surprised that all Andile's comrades spoke as though they were coming home soon. It became very clear to me that our country was truly on the verge of being liberated. The emotions raised by this knowledge were very strong.

Soon after our trip to Lusaka the homelands system started crumbling. There was much confusion among homeland leadership. Then, in February 1990, the ANC was unbanned and Nelson Mandela was released. The oppressive regime was on its way out but South Africa was far from politically stable. My dear friend Mrs Gush's only son was killed by the Ciskei police on the very day Tata Mandela was released from prison.

My family started helping with preparations for exiles to come home. We contacted the families of the first batch of returnees, as well as social workers and clergymen that might help with the transition.

Andile was among the first to come home. It was so good to have all my children in the country again. As a child, Andile was always dismantling delicate electronics like radios and small electrical appliances. At the age of nine he once took apart an expensive wall clock, wanting to know what made that tick-tock sound. After a few minutes, he reassembled the clock successfully and it carried on ticking away.

His love of electronics never went away, and during his time in exile he had studied everything and anything to do with computers and information technology. By the time he came home, he was the ANC's IT specialist, helping the party with its information systems structures.

In 1994, I felt privileged to be part of our country's first democratic elections. While I waited in the queue, I thought about the many people whose sacrifices allowed us to be where we were. I thought about my sons, who had sacrificed much and suffered greatly. I thought about Sol, standing next to me, ready to make his mark, and how much he had suffered because of his family's political involvement. I thought about my grandchildren, who would grow up in a very different country to the one my own children did.

After waiting for many hours I finally made it to the front. The officials checked my ID book, gave me a long ballot paper and showed me to the voting booth. In the tiny cubicle I looked at the photos of the many party representatives vying for the country's leadership and felt an immense sense of pride. I was finally allowed to vote, and my vote would make a difference.

# 16

So apartheid crumbled. The ANC had won the first democratic elections. It was a source of pride to see some of my fellow YWCA members included in Parliament. Andile, too, was honoured with the position of national director-general of the Department of Communications. He served the government for eight and a half years before resigning to join the private sector.

The country was free, but the struggle hadn't ended for the poor people I saw every day at the clinic and in the townships. My work was not yet done.

One day back in 1988, before I knew that Andile was alive or could guess that liberty was less than a decade away, I noticed children – some in dirty clothes, some neat and clean, as though they had just come from school – lining up side by side with work-seekers at the soup kitchen, waiting for a meal. The kitchen's organisers told me they came back in the evenings, begging for more food and a place to stay.

I spoke to the children to find out why they didn't live at home. Most of them openly shared their stories with me. Some of them were on the streets to avoid being punished for sniffing household solvents. Others were fleeing sexual and physical abuse. Their stories were frightening.

The soup kitchen was organised by an Anglican priest, Father Ed Gates, and a Mr Edward Batty. The priest was kind enough to offer the YWCA a place in the church's basement where the children could sleep overnight. We started collecting blankets and mattresses. We set up a suitable place for us to cook and for the children to wash themselves.

This was the beginning of the Daily Bread Charitable Trust. The Trust was registered in 1989, the same year I was forced to retire. Even as I was closing the door on my nursing career, the path towards a new career in childcare was unfolding before me.

We obtained the services of social workers to help us investigate the children's home situation and arrange safe homes for them. Time and again, we found that alcoholism and domestic violence had broken families to the point that their children felt they had no choice but to flee.

We also asked the Department of Education to provide us with school teachers, which they did. These teachers helped us develop a programme to help the children catch up on their education and, for those that were ready, stream back into the public school system. It was always a great source of pride for everyone involved when a child made the transition from our education programme to public school.

The first group to stay at the overnight shelter were all boys, aged between eight and fourteen. There were nine of them, their skins dirty and their clothes ragged with neglect. Among them were two boys, brothers, whose mother and father were both in jail. They had been living with relatives who spoke so poorly about their father that the boys could stand it no longer and fled.

My heart went out to these two siblings in particular. I'm not sure why. Perhaps it's because I remembered how much I worried about my children when I was detained. Perhaps it's because their loyalty to their father indicated a sense of self-worth that many of the other street children had lost.

It wasn't long before we could move the boys out of the church basement and into a house we had acquired in town. This simple step brought about a great change in the boys, especially the brothers. Their dignity had been restored, and with it their manners and happiness.

The intention was never to take these children from their parents; it was to give children an alternative to parental care that had either failed or was not available. In fact, the children's parents were encouraged to visit and see how their children were progressing.

By 1992, the number of boys had increased to the point that we needed a bigger place. With the help of an overseas donor, we bought a farm on Deerfield Road, on the way to King William's Town, not far from the East London airport.

Deerfield Road farm had a lot of old buildings that we cleaned up, painted and, where necessary, renovated to turn it into a home. The boys slept in dormitories and there were rooms for house parents. There was even a big kitchen and dining area. We used the smaller rooms as classrooms while a proper school was being built.

Meanwhile, more and more children were being accepted each month, girls as well as boys. We bought a second, smaller farm to accommodate the girls. Within a couple of years, we were taking care of more than 300 boys and sixty girls.

The Daily Bread Charitable Trust's head office remained at the house in town. This was where my office was, although I visited the homes every other day to make sure the programmes were running smoothly and to take care of any arising emergencies. By now I had recruited my old friend Mrs Gush to work on the project. She was based at Deerfield Road, doing assessments of the children to help figure out who could be referred to social services and who could be sent home.

In Xhosa there is a saying, okungapheli kuyahlola. Indeed, life is change. In 1998, after eleven years of running the Daily Bread Charitable Trust, darkness approached.

I got my first taste of what was to come during a visit to Deerfield Road. I had been called in to address a complaint. When I got there, I asked the children to assemble in the dining room so that I could address them. Usually they would respond to such a request quickly and with discipline. This time, however, only two boys responded. The rest – about 140 of them – started singing and toyi-toyiing outside.

"What's going on here?" I asked one of the house parents and Mrs Gush.

"I'm not sure," was the reply. "Some people came and spoke to them about an hour ago. They've been impossible ever since."

"Who were these people?"

Neither Mrs Gush nor the house parent knew.

"I have to go. Please tell the children I'll come back tomorrow. We can talk about this then."

I thought the outburst would have blown over by the following day, but when I got there it was worse. The children had refused to attend class or assemble for a meeting. When I went out to talk to them, they said they were unhappy about how we managed the farm. They were especially unhappy about the white people who worked for the Daily Bread Charitable Trust. They took away the keys for the car I was using.

When eventually I got away, I discovered that the same thing was happening at the girls' farm. There was chaos and protest wherever I turned, instigated by faceless accusers and carried out by children who had been appreciative of their care just days before.

Two days later, the children marched on the Daily Bread's head office in town, armed with placards, toyi-toyiing and singing all the way. The crowd was unmanageable. Among them were a handful of adults wearing union T-shirts.

The situation at Daily Bread was becoming unstable. As a safety measure, Mrs Gush moved her office from the children's home to my office in town. The managing committee met to resolve the crisis, but we couldn't agree on a way forward. I felt confused. I had always believed that conflict and misunderstandings could be democratically resolved, but this was bullying, against which there is no argument.

By this time I was almost seventy years old. I was tired of fighting. All I wanted was peace, so I decided to remove myself from the troubled situation that had become the Daily Bread. Mrs Gush left the Daily Bread at the same time, both because of the union trouble and because her health was starting to fail. She had been unwell for some time by the time she stopped working at the end of November 1998. By the time I visited her early the following month, her condition had worsened. She died on the morning of 13 December. I missed her deeply for many years, and even today struggle to contain my impulse to mother her children, knowing how much she loved her two daughters after she lost her only son.

By the end of 1998 I was emotionally exhausted. I had lost one of the best friends I would ever know and watched something I had worked so hard to build be taken from me.

I decided to let the Daily Bread go and focus on the future. During my career, I had nursed babies between the ages of ten days and two years. The street children I worked with tended to be older, between the ages of eight and eighteen, most often young teenagers. I felt I was ready to focus on younger children, between the ages of two and six.

By now Sol and I had sold our house in Gompo township and bought a bigger one in a suburb of East London called Amalinda. The Amalinda house had lots of space, and the path that presented itself to me now was to open a day-care centre to provide the children of Duncan Village with a stimulating home environment and dedicated caregivers that would help plant the seeds for their future development during those all-important preschool years.

I completed a childcare course with the Department of Health and researched East London care centres. Sol and I renovated our house to convert the garage and car port into two classrooms with lovely big windows, and closed up our huge verandah to create a bathroom and an area where the children could play on rainy days. Outside we installed swings, a jungle gym and a sand pit, ready for little fingers and toes. Sol even built some furniture designed for little people.

By February 1999, the Laugh and Learn Educare Centre was ready to receive its first intake. At first we only accepted 25 children. It wasn't long before the demand for the school grew to the point that I had to hire two new teachers. Sol and I also decided to move out, into another house, so that the whole Amalinda house could be used as a school. One of the sitting rooms was turned into a classroom and the other prepared for use as a computer lab.

In February 2009, I was blessed to be part of a programme called Second Chance Youth Skills, which aimed to give young men and women a "second chance" in life by giving them the work skills they would need to become gainfully employed. I served as the founding committee's treasurer for three years, during which time I helped find a suitable venue for training.

Laugh and Learn is still going, helping to develop little minds, bodies and spirits. In 2012, to my surprise and delight, I received a visit from the two young brothers who had tugged at my heart when the Daily Bread first started. Their neighbour happened to be a parent of one of my students. We spoke, and they told me about their lives. The older brother had gone on to become a taxi driver, while the younger – who was thirty years old by now – had a tertiary education and was working at Haga Haga hotel in Alice. They both looked smart and mature, and I felt proud to have helped them along their journey.

I firmly believe that the crèche is playing a part, however small, in helping to build a better country. We teach the little ones self-reliance and prepare the older ones for "big school". We teach all the children in their mother tongue, using indigenous games and dances, while also teaching them English. This gives them confidence in expressing themselves. We must be doing something right, because many of our former pupils, now adults and parents themselves, have brought their children to us. Unfortunately I began this centre late in life and my own grandchildren did not have the opportunity to attend.

Every time I watch these happy, innocent children, playing around my old home, a warm feeling of gratitude fills my heart. On occasion, when I am lucky, one of them will hug me around my knees with those short little arms and say, "I love you, Makhulu wam."

# 17

Now, as I write this, I am eighty-four years old. My family now is different to what it was when I was a young girl. My parents and brothers are all dead, but I have twenty-two grandchildren and eight great-grandchildren. My sister Olga is ninety-six years old. She lost her eyesight four years ago. We still talk about our life at Cala as though it was yesterday.

My children have brought me such pride and happiness, although my heart aches for Tammie, my firstborn child, who died in October 2005 at the age of fifty-four. He had TB and meningitis but chose to rely on traditional rather than western medicines. I still miss his deep voice and powerful, loud laughter at family gatherings.

My soulmate, Sol, passed away in January 2013. The hole he has left in my heart will never heal. I still plant carnations and roses in my garden. Carnations are especially dear to me because when they are finished growing, instead of shedding their petals they fold inwards, protecting the growing new seeds.

Before he passed, Sol wrote a chapter for this book. It is about knowing me through all the stages of my life – the four Ms, as we called it. He knew me as Manse, the young woman; as Mama, the mother to his children; as MaHlongwane, which is my clan name and speaks to my role as a community worker; and as Makhulu, a grandmother and advisor.

Thank you for your trust, your love and your words, Sol. I will always love you.

*I am Bro Sol, as called by the writer.*

*Manse at twenty was tall and slender. I first saw her at the Butterworth train station. What I saw never left my mind. Fortunately, six months later I recognised her at the nurse's home at Frere Hospital.*

*At thirty, she was Mama to five of my children. At the same time she was my dance partner and a reliable, loving wife to me. By forty she was Mama to our six children, of which three were already boarding at high school and the rest were at home, close to their parents' love and helping us weave ladies' bags for our family business.*

*At fifty, she was MaHlongwane, the community worker. By now all the children were at high school or studying at college or university. As parents, we faced a lot of challenges due to political turmoil. The children's education was disrupted by detentions and even going into exile.*

*At sixty, we were both forced to retire unexpectedly after she spent a year in detention, together with two of our sons. We had to reorganise our lives to adjust to the situation, working very hard to meet our financial needs.*

*At seventy, she was Makhulu, grandmother. By now we had overcome all our obstacles and were enjoying a loving environment in a comfortable home, surrounded by our older grandchildren and about fifty innocent young children placed in our care by their parents. Happiness and laughter at its best.*

*Makhulu at eighty is taking things easy, moving around slowly, watering her flower garden, all the while carrying a pen and paper. She is telling everyone that her book will be on the shelves by the time she turns eighty-three. I honestly believe her, because of her strength. Yes, I know all her four M's well.*

# PART 2 LIFE LESSONS

"MaHlongwane grew up in less than favourable conditions. All she knew was struggle. Today, however, she has overcome these many challenges and stands strong, living proof that if she can make it, so can anyone."

– Nomzi Beni, niece

I am now eighty-four years old. In my years on this Earth, people have come to me for advice on many things. Perhaps it was because I was a nurse, and they hoped that I could make them feel better. Possibly it was because I was a mature soul, and at my age you are expected to know a thing or two. Perhaps it is because they look at my successful children and think that I must have done something right in raising them. Possibly my work in the community showed people that I was the type of person who cared and would listen. And listen I did – not just to people's problems, but to the themes that emerged in people's lives, time and again.

In some ways, the problems that people have come to me with are the same as those faced by people throughout the world: how can I be a better wife and mother? How can I be a better husband and father? How can I keep my family together when there are so many social forces pulling us apart? However, because of our history, our geography and our traditions, South Africans face a set of challenges that few other nations do. Certainly, few Americans struggle with the question of how to combine their traditional identities with their western, professional lives. And no other country has had to overcome the psychological wounds of apartheid and the effects it had on our self-esteem and economic opportunities.

I haven't always had answers for these people. All I know is that there can be no solution to any problem if someone doesn't possess self-knowledge, self-assurance and self-sufficiency. Developing these things requires a sincere commitment. Certain attitudes, behaviours and thought patterns can help show the way.

There is no one-size-fits-all solution in life, and I do not wish to pretend that there is. However, I do know that I am a woman, a mother, a professional and an African, and what has worked for me and my family may also work for yours. Here are some of the solutions I have found for myself, applied in raising my family and helped others discover for themselves.

Much of what is written here is directed at young people and women as wives, mothers and professionals, although I have also put down my thoughts on what I think it means to be an honourable man and husband. It is true that I will never be a man or a husband, but I have had enough sons and have been married enough years to have an idea of the troubles that men face. So please indulge an old woman who has spent her life caring for and loving men of all ages.

I hope my discoveries can help you find your path more clearly and guide you in asking the kinds of questions that will help you find answers.

"My mother taught me many lessons, some of which she picked up from the books she was always reading, some of which she learnt from living her life. These are the ones I still hold closest to my heart as they are the basis of what it means to be human:
- Put things where you found them
- Clean up your own mess
- Don't take things that are not yours
- Say you are sorry when you hurt someone
- Share everything you have
- Wash hands before you eat
- Never consciously tell a lie
- Greet all people with a smile
- Respect young and old
- Live contentedly with small means
- Never indulge in self-destruction
- Be happy and live life to the full
- Face problems head on."

— Nomhamha, daughter

# ON TRIBALISM IN SOUTH AFRICA

We are all aware of the tribal root systems that exist within the fibre of our country, and the divisions they cause in us as a nation. We have all had the experience where, on addressing a stranger in one's own language, that person responds with anger, saying, "I don't speak your language. I only speak my own language."

People seem to believe that their tribal affiliations run deeper than, say, their affiliations with their countrymen. But the fact is, such strong tribal alliance is a relatively new thing. Those who are old enough will remember that, in the days before freedom, tribal affiliation was not a matter of consequence at all. The glue that held us together was our shared experience of oppression and our united opposition to apartheid. Very, very rarely did anyone ask about tribal affiliations. We saw and regarded ourselves as simply African. This is why we resisted the Bantustan policy – because we disliked how it boxed in our identity.

With freedom, we lost this approach to our humanity. Since 1994, class and tribal distinctions have been growing in the population's psyche. We have started to stratify ourselves into different cultural and class groups. We now have the "Black Diamond" class of successful African entrepreneurs; the izikhotane, young people who demonstrate how much money they have by burning expensive items; and many other groupings and gangs that have only emerged in the past two decades.

I don't think the stratification of society into interest and tribal groups is, in itself, a problem. It only becomes a problem when we begin to see ourselves as belonging to a particular cultural group before we identify ourselves as being South African. We have eleven official languages in this country. That translates to at least eleven tribal groupings, each with its own traditions and cultural knowledge. We will never be able to create a South African identity that draws equally from all these groupings. It is just not possible.

What we need is to understand that we are all first and foremost South Africans. It is only once we all regard ourselves as one and the same in our South Africanness that our true identity will be able to emerge. I personally like to think of myself as a South African who is Xhosa, and not the other way around. As it is, the country is turning into a hodge-podge of racial and tribal groupings that are growing further from each other rather than together under the common goal of developing this beautiful country of ours.

## ASK YOURSELF

What is the difference between being a South African who belongs to a tribe and a tribesman who is also South African? Do you gain anything by primarily aligning yourself with your own tribe, to the exclusion of others? Could you gain something by first being a South African, and then a member of your tribe?

No one can change the country of your birth. Even if you move abroad, nothing can change the fact that you were born in South Africa, just like no one can change the fact that you were born to a particular tribe. The only difference is the size of your "family": you share your South Africanness with other tribes, whereas you share your tribal affiliation only with your fellow tribe members.

# 2

## ON RAISING A FAMILY

Parents occupy a powerful position in shaping the calibre and quality of their families. In Xhosa we say the mother is "intsika yom'zi", the foundation stone of the home. Mothers and fathers both have a special role to play in providing structures and systems to ensure that their families run smoothly.

Why is a well-run family important? Because it is where happy, successful, self-realised individuals are born, and happy, successful, self-realised individuals create a strong, self-sufficient, successful nation. The type of country we are depends directly on the quality of each citizen's family life, which in turn is affected by the efforts of the parents, the grandparents and other family members. Together, therefore, the nation's parents steer the spiritual, material, physical and emotional life of the country.

I believe that a powerful and prosperous family is one in which both parents and the extended family are rooted in the teachings of the Lord. Spiritual awareness of God gives one personal power. Teaching one's children the principles of godly living is the door to prosperity.

The worst thing you can do for your children is to confuse prosperity with materialism. In today's South Africa it is common for both parents to be educated and have careers. They go out to work, not only to express their individualism, but also to jointly provide a better life for their children. Mothers depend on housekeepers to complete household chores like cooking and looking after the children.

"A few times I overhead my father saying to my mother, 'Manse, you have done a wonderful job bringing up these children.'

My mother would reply, 'It was a long journey, Bro Sol. I wouldn't have been able to walk it without you.'

These are the best words any child could hear from their parent's lips. My mother taught me that we all need to love and be loved. We need people to tell us that we are special, irreplaceable. We need people who will attend to our needs and remove our fears and insecurities, the way our parents did when we were small. Most of all, we need to love those who love us.

Mama, I have always tried to make you proud. I may have failed here and there, but I have tried and am still trying. I thank you from the bottom of my heart for all you've done for me. I bless the Lord for giving me the best mother there could be."

– Linda, youngest son

While I believe this is necessary if both parents are to have a career, when taken to extremes it can have a severely detrimental effect on parenting. Too many parents don't make the time to help their children with their homework or listen to their problems. Instead, they put a bandage over the emotional gap growing between themselves and their offspring by buying their children expensive clothes and gadgets. An iPhone is no substitute for love. The attention a parent gives – or withholds from – a child is irreplaceable and crucial for that child to develop a sense of self-worth.

Before long, parents realise that their children have grown up without them. They have been too busy to watch their children grow. They themselves haven't grown up enough to realise that merely providing food and clothes and money is not enough. Too few parents even bother to ask what their children spend money on; they simply hand it over to get the child out of their hair.

Our children are our future. They need us to invest our time and energy and thought into creating systems and greater context that will make them feel safe and allow them to grow and prosper from childhood to adulthood. They need us to be there for them, both physically and emotionally, and they need us to know how to say "no". This is the only way children can grow up whole and balanced.

Many parents would love to spend more time with their children, but feel broken by the pressures of society. The modern world is highly competitive, driving even loving parents to set their children aside so that they can meet the never-ending demands of work. It is easy for the amount of time mothers and fathers spend with their children to diminish to the point where they end up being part-time parents.

I believe that part-time parenting can be avoided by skilfully budgeting time. Give yourself the space to be a parent by allowing yourself to achieve your career goals at a more reasonable pace. There is no benefit to reaching the top of the corporate ladder by thirty if it comes at the cost of spending time with your children. There is nothing wrong with obtaining a degree or achieving a promotion at thirty-five or even forty, and the benefits of being there for your children, especially when they are young, will be reaped for the rest of your life.

## ASK YOURSELF

Do I have confidence in my ability as a parent? Do I value the lessons I learnt growing up, and can I build on them? Do I respect the values of my culture so that I am free to be my own person as a parent? Do I have faith in my Creator, who supports my efforts?

Am I making enough time to be with my children in a meaningful way? What will part-time parenting do to my relationship with my children later on? Is there any way I can budget my time better to create space to be with my children?

When I was raising my family, a parent's word was non-negotiable and used as a tool to guide children into adulthood. Our culture was very strong and powerful norms were maintained. The modern move to assimilate western culture has, in some ways, had a negative impact on our child-rearing practices. Lessons learnt on television, easy access to drugs and the permissiveness of society often hinder parents who try to instil sober principles of self-control and good behaviour in their children.

Effective time management doesn't only mean managing your time on a day-to-day basis. It also means managing your time from decade to decade with the understanding that a smaller child needs more parental attention than an older child, while education and a career trajectory are ongoing throughout life. I believe it is important to constantly reassess how you manage your time.

*Notes*

# 3

## ON BEING A WIFE

I believe women have the power to influence their families' emotional tenor. They have the ability to create happiness as well as unhappiness and strife in their homes.

I believe that, in a happy marriage, the husband works to provide while the woman works to create a harmonious, happy home (even if she also works to provide). Each partner sees and appreciates the efforts of the other. Darkness creeps in when one party isn't satisfied with the efforts of the other and accusations start to fly. These accusations cause guilt, guilt encourages loneliness, loneliness makes one unhappy and unhappiness threatens marital unity to the point of one partner seeking happiness elsewhere.

I was once a young wife too, and I have seen many young wives struggle with the same things I did when I was young. I believe that the source of love is deep, and often all it takes is one word, one action, one thought to reduce your spouse's suffering and return to joy.

When I speak to young women experiencing marital strife, I like to remind them of a few things:

- If your husband chose to marry you, he was not forced.
- If he admires your friend's dress, he might want to give you a similar one.
- If his meeting was supposed to end at 8 pm and he comes home at 10 pm, he was not the chairperson.
- If he complains about a nagging secretary at the office, do not give him a nagging wife at home.
- If he does not finish his dinner, it is possible that there is a restaurant near the car wash he used on his way home.

- If he is quiet because he is upset, it might have nothing to do with you.
- If he gives his secretary a lift home, it might have been because of the bad weather.
- If your neighbour warns you about your husband, she can just as easily warn him about you.
- If his smile is broad when seeing the housekeeper, perhaps it's because she packs his bag so neatly.
- If he says he forgot to pay for electricity, your brother forgets too.
- If you throw his dinner plate down in front of him in anger, only the dog understands body language.
- If your mother-in-law whispers when talking to her son, your mother goes with you to the bathroom to talk to you.
- If you excuse yourself when you make a mistake, your husband too needs to be excused.
- If you lied to cool down your neighbour, your husband can lie to cool you down too.

In short, if you have realised that you are not perfect like everybody else, your husband is just like everybody else too. To belittle and accuse him will only result in avoidance and lies. Rather believe him and be understanding. Inject some humour when commenting on his shortcomings, if you feel you absolutely have to: if his shoes are dirty, blame the mud, and if he comes home late, blame the watch. Make giving a way of life.

I believe in the power of women. Women are strong, emotionally and mentally, and have the tolerance, compassion and understanding to adapt to any situation. To empower a young woman to have patience and control over her thoughts is to help her achieve her dreams in creating a happy family. Is that not what we all wish for?

## ASK YOURSELF

When you are upset with each other, do you stew quietly, or have you learnt to communicate effectively? Have you learnt to say, "This is how I am feeling"? Have you learnt to respect your partner for being open about their feelings?

How do you resolve conflict? Do you wait until you have a quiet moment together, or do you fly off the cuff there and then? How much do you value honesty with each other? Do you show understanding and empathy, or do you sit in judgment? Do you speak to each other in a manner that fosters respect?

Effective communication in a marriage is honest, non-accusatory and non-judgmental. It is, in a word, respectful. That isn't always easy to achieve, especially when you and your spouse disagree, but there can be no positive outcome when words are said with disrespect.

Many couples struggle to speak openly about finances and their views of their family's future. These are emotionally charged subjects that easily trigger accusations and scorn. Learn to get in touch with your feelings around these subjects and examine whether these feelings are reasonable. If they are, focus on communicating your position with respect, bearing in mind that your partner may have equally reasonable beliefs that do not concur.

A strong marriage is one where both partners empower each other. Some spouses seem to find pleasure in belittling their partners as a way to feel better about themselves. A more productive and effective approach would be for them to work on developing confidence about themselves instead. Yes, you are allowed to acknowledge your achievements. Knowing who you are doesn't make you proud or boastful.

# 4

## ON BALANCING PROFESSIONALISM AND TRADITIONALISM

Because we no longer learn by oral tradition, we are losing important knowledge about many of our cultural practices. The best way to preserve this knowledge is to write down those processes that are important to us and we would like to maintain, both for our own use and for the benefit of future generations. For example, what is the imbeleko ceremony, and how is it done? Why and how is the ten-day reclusion period, ukubasefukwini, observed? And what is the ritual to accept a bride into her new home? In a society where increasing tribalism is dividing the country, it might even help prevent further division in future by providing a written, definitive reference as to how certain traditional practices are carried out.

An issue I have seen many people struggle with, and one that I myself had to manage with care, is how to balance one's professional and cultural life. Traditional and professional roles are often in direct conflict with each other, leaving young people – especially young women and mothers – with the feeling that they have to choose one or the other.

Let's describe this person, the woman facing this conflict: she is a working mother, highly educated and skilled, a powerful corporate executive, entrepreneur or a recognised expert in her field. She is aspirational and sophisticated, classy and feminine. She works hard to be successful in different areas in her life. She knows that the best thing that she can do for herself and her family is to be the working person, wife and mother that she is.

At the same time, she is an African woman, an African mother. She is expected to be a good African wife who prepares and serves her husband and children's meals and meets all their other domestic needs. She is expected to raise her own children and carefully nurture strong connections with the greater family and clan. Especially when she first becomes a wife, she is expected to prepare and serve the food, make tea and otherwise convincingly take the role of being a good makoti – often without fully understanding what her husband's family expects of her, especially if she herself doesn't come from a very traditional background.

How does this woman bridge the gap between the sophisticated, powerful businessperson she is in her professional life and the African woman married into a traditional family in her private life? It may be tempting to disregard the traditional ways altogether, but in the long term, that would only result in strife with, and isolation from, the greater family. It has been my sad experience to see family members at loggerheads regarding traditional rituals like the way we bury our dead, which has been so coloured by western culture that it would seem we are denying our roots. Yes, culture is an object of change. We may tweak things here and there, but we shouldn't throw away the fundamentals. At the end of the day, we may live in the suburbs but we are still Africans. We should uphold our traditions and culture as much as we can.

> "Mamkhulu is a true mother, a nurturer, a caregiver. Her warmth and compassion is felt through generations that have benefited from her wisdom and comfort. I am grateful to have had Mamkhulu in my life, and for everything she taught me as a young lady: to be a leader and never a follower, to stay true to myself, my culture and my family principles. May God continue to bless her with more years with us."
>
> – Hlathikazi Beni, grand-niece

I believe that openness and mutual communication is the only way to overcome these tensions and conflicts. Young professional women should try not to disregard traditional ways out of hand – they have their place, they are the glue that keeps extended families and clans together.

At the same time, older matriarchs need to realise that young women live in a very different world to the one they grew up in. They might not immediately know what is expected of them when they marry into a traditional family. So, rather than confront a new makoti for not wearing a headscarf or coming to a funeral with lots of make-up and a short skirt, they should identify a time to sit down with her and talk her through the various processes and practices of her new extended family. As a woman coming into her husband's family, it will be her responsibility to pass these cultural values and norms on to her children and their spouses one day. She will not be able to do this without help.

## ASK YOURSELF

Which family rituals and traditions have meaning for you? Do you have a written record of these traditions? What is the best way to communicate these traditions to new members of your family in a welcoming, encouraging way?

We Africans have a very good practice called *ukuyala* that is still largely practised to this day, even in very westernised families. This takes place at the ceremony when the bride is being accepted into her husband's home. It is an opportunity for the matriarchs on her side of the family to advise her how to be a good wife. I believe it is also an opportunity for matriarchs on the husband's side to teach the makoti about the expectations, taboos and rituals of the family into which she is marrying. Having a written record of a family's traditions might help clearly communicate these issues too.

# 5

## ON BEING A MAN

I have met many men, especially young men, who struggle with a great deal of anger and frustration. They feel as though their problems are insurmountable and they are helpless to change their fates. They don't know who to blame and sometimes they end up lashing out at those closest to them, creating much unhappiness for themselves and their loved ones.

I believe the problems that these men face, while real, are made worse when they react with frustration and anger. Eventually, this reaction becomes more of a problem than the original obstacle ever was. These men are, in effect, falling into traps of their own making.

To make matters worse they then start associating with other youngsters who are equally angry. These men start feeding off each other's dissatisfactions, goading each other to act out their anger. Before long, they believe that the best possible way to solve a problem and reclaim some power in their lives is to lie, strike out or steal.

I believe men who follow such a path will never find happiness, because they are not honouring themselves. The pillars of strength for a young man are accountability, responsibility and respect. These can only be achieved if these men learn to accept their feelings of anger and find more constructive ways of dealing with it.

This cannot be achieved in the heat of the moment. It takes practice. If a young man comes to me, distressed at how he has hit his wife or abused drugs to escape his problems, I give him this exercise to do: sit comfortably for a few minutes, focusing on the rhythm of your breathing. Think back over the past few hours or days, looking for an incident where you reacted with anger or frustration. It may be that someone took your parking space in front of you, or someone was late to pick you up for work. Focus on the incident and how it made you feel. Think about possible reasons the incident took place. Perhaps the person who took your parking spot didn't see you, or was in a terrible rush. Perhaps your work colleague got stuck in traffic. Now let go of that irritation and think about other ways to respond instead.

Remember, men are the protectors of society. At some stage, your family's security may depend on you. A protector should at all times be level-headed and have self-control, because uncontrolled anger could have serious consequences.

## ASK YOURSELF

What happens in your psyche when you hit a woman, lie unnecessarily, blame someone else for your mistakes, or fail to uphold a promise? Do you feel more powerful and in control? Does the feeling last?

There comes a time when everyone, man or woman, needs to decide what kind of person he or she wants to be. If you look in the mirror, do you see the kind of man you want to be? If not, ask yourself how you plan to become a better person, both to create a better life for yourself and to contribute more constructively to your community. Take the wildest of your dreams and start working towards that. This includes fortifying your life with the right friendships.

# 6

## ON BEING A FATHER

With being a father comes the responsibility of the physical, emotional and spiritual well-being of your children. It is the father's duty to see to it that there is a home for his family. It is he who provides the necessary essentials – food, clothing, access to education and guidance. My husband, Bra Sol, was exemplary in this respect. It pains me to see so many young mothers queuing up for grant money to feed their children. I always ask myself, "Where are the fathers?" It is the father's duty to support the mother, provide for the children and help raise them.

The preparation for manhood should begin at an early age. A boy should know that his chores will be a little heavier than those given to a girl. In traditional society, it was expected of boys to chop wood, herd cattle and do the garden while girls prepared food and tended the fire. Young men grew up knowing that they were going to be men. This was not to teach men to be chauvinistic; it was to teach them to appreciate their role.

Today's society emphasises equality, but does not say much about the different expectations of each sex. I believe this contributes to society's problems. My Mamkhulu taught us that, while we were equal and she loved us all, she had different expectations of the boys and the girls in her house. This is the psychological stance we need to develop in our young men: that while men and women are equal, we have different roles to play in creating a society of equality and justice.

It is unacceptable for a young man, for a husband, to raise his hand to his sister or wife. Today we see a lot of abuse. What is missing in the emotional code of men who do this? Could it be that they are lacking the sense that they are society's protectors?

## ASK YOURSELF

What is the father's role in the family? How can a father ensure that his son becomes a responsible, respectful, dignified man?

Today's fathers often cede their responsibilities in the home to mothers, undermining their family's cohesion by not recognising that theirs is a role that can only be played by a father. It is the father's role to govern the home and establish rules for how things should be done in the family. The father who does this in a manner that is loving, attentive, trusting and respectful to his wife and children is, by example, showing his sons how to be men. It was my husband's trust that built me up and made me the mother that I am today. For that I am eternally grateful.

*Notes*

# 7

## ON HOW TECHNOLOGY IS AFFECTING WOMEN

Technology affects every aspect of our lives today. For women in particular, it influences our reproductive lives, our careers and our responsibilities in the home.

When I went to hospital to deliver my second-born child, I didn't know that I would be delivering twins. The first baby came out, perfect delivery. Sol and I were ecstatic. Sol went home, leaving me to rest, but instead of resting I went into labour again. What a surprise for Sol when he came to visit the following day and found me with not one baby but two!

Had there been the technology that we have today, I would have known long before my due date that I was expecting twins. The risks of carrying and delivering twins could have been mitigated well in advance. As it is, I am grateful there were no complications.

Technology has an extraordinary ability to help people attain a better quality of life in every aspect, from medicine to education. Maternal and child mortality have improved immeasurably, and online learning is taking formal education to girls and women who would otherwise not have had the opportunity.

> "'Aspire to be like Mount Fuji, with such a broad and solid foundation that the strongest earthquake cannot move you, and so tall that the greatest enterprises of common men seem insignificant from your lofty perspective. With your mind as high as Mount Fuji, you can see all things clearly. And you can see all the forces that shape events, not just the things happening near to you.'

This quote, from Japanese swordsman Miyamoto Musashi, says it all when it comes to what Makhulu did for our families. The

Laugh and Learn Educare Centre has given our children such a solid foundation, it is almost impossible to shake. Their self-image is well established, having been groomed and nurtured by Makhulu and the values embedded in this wonderful centre of learning."
– Vuyo Sidelo, chairperson of Laugh and Learn Educare Centre board member and family friend

Over the decades, technology has also released women from the time commitment of their daily household responsibilities, enabling them to pursue careers and an education. At the turn of the twentieth century, women's lives consisted of simple home-based activities. They were the homemakers, having children, cooking meals and, in African societies, fetching wood and water and building huts.

The next generation, that of my mother, moved up the technology scale. While very much still homemakers, they bought sewing machines to make their own clothes, installed water pumps and used modern coal stoves and oil lamps instead of cooking over an open fire and using candles.

My generation moved up the scale a little more. Most of us were able to get an education and become nurses or teachers, although you could count on one hand the women who were doctors, lawyers and social workers. Very, very few women of my generation learnt how to drive.

This changed by the next generation. My daughter's generation, further freed from domestic activities by dishwashers and vacuum cleaners, entered the halls of the corporate world. While many women of her generation didn't manage to crack the glass ceiling, they nonetheless touched it. For both of us, education, westernisation and politicisation improved our quality of life.

Now, in the twenty-first century, women can enter any kind of work. They can become CEOs of companies. There are woman presidents in Africa – Liberia and Malawi being notable firsts. Women are taking up leadership positions as scientists, inventors and space explorers.

Technology has even changed the most fundamental aspect of being a woman: pregnancy and motherhood. These days, you may choose to become a mother by natural fertilisation or by artificial fertilisation methods. You could even choose to use the kind services of a surrogate mother. Increasingly, technology is giving women the option to have a child without involving their own bodies or having to form a family unit with a father or male figure.

Does this bode well for the family of the future? In the future, will we even have an institution called the family? As technology keeps taking strides, we have to be aware of the real possibility that co-parenting with men may become obsolete. What is to stop a high-powered woman from ordering her children from a particular gene pool and employing the services of a surrogate mother to bring them into the world?

I believe women should take the time to carefully consider the effect of technology on their lives as mothers, wives and nurturers of families. While some technologies have indubitably liberated women, others, like social media, have the potential to dominate freed-up time and attention that would be better spent helping one's children finish their homework or cooking a decent meal. Technology is powerful, but it needs to be managed with care.

## ASK YOURSELF

How can I use technology to improve my quality of life or realise my potential? Is there any way technology is standing in the way of being a good parent, spouse or worker? Do I ever stop to consider the consequences of using a new technology, or do I simply use it because it's there? Is the technology in control, or am I?

Technology is, in itself, neither good nor bad. Too often, society's ethical development lags behind technological developments, and technological advances become widespread before their effect has been carefully considered. For instance, it is presently possible for a woman to have a child by herself, without a man's involvement. But is it desirable? Parenting is incredibly time-consuming when two parents are involved; will a child get enough attention and guidance when there is only one parent, who is both the main caregiver and provider? These and other questions should be considered before any reproductive decisions are made. Similarly, the consequences of a new technology should be closely examined before it is adopted.

*Notes*

# 8

## ON CREATING A SENSE OF BELONGING

Our sense of belonging stems from the understanding that we are part of something larger than ourselves. For most of us, the first larger structure we are exposed to is our extended family.

Extended families today are under siege. The closeness of years gone by has diminished. Sundays used to be when families would gather for lunch at the grandmother's house, giving grown-up siblings the opportunity to touch base and cousins the chance to play together. A strong feeling and sense of family was maintained. I know people who don't have this family experience, even in our African society. Grandmothers sit alone in their flats or old-age homes on Sundays. They have very little communication with their families, who often live far away. This is a bad situation indeed – one that is entirely unnecessary and incredibly destructive for the sense of belonging in young and old alike.

My family is scattered throughout South Africa and the world, yet we routinely have family meetings attended by members from all generations. This presents an opportunity for everyone to speak to each other face to face – such an important (and often overlooked) element in this technological age of ours.

> "Mamkhulu's presence in my life has made me into the woman I am today. She made me realise that, if I love myself, it will be easier to love those around me. She planted a sense of belonging in the empty space in my heart."
>
> – Linda Lavisa, granddaughter

Families should also try to develop a deeper understanding of their particular traditional practices and beliefs. I have seen families torn apart because some family members approach life from a traditional perspective while others emphasise the spiritual. I believe that parents, and mothers in particular, play a role in handing down beliefs, customs and traditions in a meaningful, unified way so as to preserve their strength and ensure future cohesion in families. If we teach our young ones as they grow up, they will, in turn, teach their own children. We need that generational teaching to preserve our heritage.

All this takes effective, compassionate communication. First and foremost, good communicators know themselves. They know what kind of person they are, their strengths and their weaknesses. They are patient – or learn to develop patience – without which communication is impossible. It is only though effective communication that we can bring harmony and understanding to our families and our relationships.

## ASK YOURSELF

Do I have a real sense of belonging to something bigger than myself? Do my children? What can I do to better connect with members of the extended family?

Our family is large and varied. No two members are the same, yet we share a sense of unity and belonging that most families today don't.

This kind of unity doesn't happen by accident. We make an effort. My family regularly holds family meetings – three-day gatherings that all members of the family are expected to attend – with a formal agenda to discuss arising issues and communicate information.

I believe all families would benefit from such events, which are an important platform to express mutual support, for bonding and for creating a sense of belonging to something bigger than oneself.

# 9

## ON CREATING A LEGACY

I believe a family is much like a business in that it consists of individuals who lead their own lives but are united by a common goal.

In a business, that common goal is to create a product or provide a service to generate profits for the benefit of all employees.

In a family, that common goal is less defined. It can be based on love alone, or it can include more concrete goals such as providing for future generations.

The reason many families don't pursue goals as a group is because of the high emotional content that often comes with family interactions. Sibling rivalry, spousal disagreements, jealousy between cousins – all these factors come into play when families get together.

I believe families can benefit from running themselves along the same lines as a business, right down to having a vision, a mission and a formal constitution. Sol and I did this in running our family. Today, I am a great-grandmother. More than two generations have been added to the collective and we are still largely united in pursuing our values of knowledge, caring and unity. We are also working to create a legacy of intellectual, emotional and practical wealth for the generations to come. It is my hope that future generations of the Ngcaba family will build upon these achievements.

# ASK YOURSELF

Would my extended family benefit from being run as a business? Which business practices would be useful in my family today?

My family has designed its own coat of arms. We have a mission statement and a vision. We even have a family constitution that goes into specifics about, for instance, our family's attitude towards adoption and surrogate parenting (we are open to both) and mechanisms for managing family conflict (we set up an independent conflict-resolution committee that acts as mediator to the conflict).

We go to great lengths to promote our family's cohesion. This is necessary if we are to enjoy the full benefits of operating as a group, such as collective bargaining for medical aid or household insurance and organising workshops to collectively help the youngsters in our family come to terms with "adult" issues such as buying a car, getting married and paying income tax.

We are aware that it is important for everyone to feel invested in such a family structure, so we always try to involve all members of the extended family when making decisions, initiating projects or amending our constitution, as we need to do in a constantly changing world.

For those who are interested, I have provided a copy of my family's constitution at the end of this book. Readers are welcome to adapt this for their family as they see fit. It's a lot of work, but the benefits of formalising such structures are real and will be felt for generations to come.

# AFTERWORD

I come from the storms, the winds, the frost, the piercing thorns, the thundering skies of the Eastern Cape. I am the product of the deaths and separations that have left deep scars on my heart. Marriage and children have lightened my spirit, though, and I have come to realise that life's ups and downs grow and strengthen us.

I also come from love – my mother's love, my father's love, the love of my brothers and sisters. I come from the love and trust of my husband, my children, my family and my friends. Above all, love is the key. Let us try to give love and do what we do, with love. That is the most important ingredient for success.

Once you are able to trust, you are on your way towards a long-lasting relationship, whether with your children or your husband. The trust Sol and I had carried us through challenging times. Trust was the impetus we needed to achieve our ambitions.

Self-knowledge and self-respect are also important. Regularly evaluate your strengths and weaknesses, then face the problems that need to be solved instead of running away or shifting the blame to others. If you endeavour to be honest about who you are and the situation you are in, you may be able to accommodate the present and the future.

Let prayer be an important source of strength for your family. In days gone by, we Africans began and ended the day with prayer. That was our solace and our strength.

If you are a mother or a father, cultivate strong family roots. Make your home a haven of love for your partner and your offspring. Teach your children strong moral values so that they will be able to reach higher.

Learn to listen to your children. Sometimes when our children speak to us, our minds are far away, worrying about work deadlines or bond repayments. Yes, they will always argue with us but it is not for us to ignore what they are saying. Remember, children today live a stressful life. The social pressures to conform are tremendous. Drugs are easily available. They are also attracted to the virtual world of Facebook and Twitter, which is appealing, but is really no cure for the emptiness and pain caused by absent parents.

Equally, people should learn to be involved with their communities. Duncan Village used to be the home of many prominent people, professionals such as lawyers, doctors and successful businesspeople. Where are they today? They are contributing their services elsewhere, where life is more lucrative. A pity, but life has to go on. It bothers me, though. Why it is that we African people no longer have our own prestigious schools? Our children go to schools like Hilton and St David's. Are our children being taught to honour who they are and where they come from?

We must never forget our roots, especially our rural backgrounds. Those who can, owe it to families back home to help with the upkeep of the family home. It was always my husband's greatest wish to renovate his rural home. As his partner and his wife, I encouraged him to do so. After many years, the house was complete. When his mother retired, she was able to do so with dignity in a comfortable home. His sister and her children were able to live there too. To this day, when I have the time, I thoroughly enjoy going back to this home, even for a few days.

After living in Duncan Village for thirty-two years, Sol and I moved to Gompo township a few kilometres away. Later, we took out a mortgage bond and bought ourselves a bigger, nicer home at Amalinda that would be able to accommodate all our children and grandchildren when they came to visit. Many African people view a move to the suburbs negatively. My only response is that we should all accept that change comes with new opportunities and responsibilities. Where we could not buy land or own our own home before, now we could. And why not? My seventieth birthday was celebrated in this new home, and five of my grandsons were welcomed from traditional school there. As a family, we hold regular family workshops there. It has been the venue of much love, laughter and joy.

It is the express duty and responsibility of parents to engender in their children a passion for education as a vehicle for stability and prosperity. Our country is short of critical skills, especially technological skills. I get discouraged when I ask a child, "What are you studying at university?" Almost invariably the answer is some or other soft skill. There are very few children who take up challenging careers where maths, science and physics are central. Why should parents go through the pain of educating their children, only to have their children sit at home vegetating because the area of work is oversubscribed?

Our society is burdened by extreme inequality. Yes, this is a legacy of the apartheid years, but the government now has the power to correct these problems. We need to come together as a nation to find ways to overcome the land question in particular. This is going to be the source of a lot of destabilisation in the country.

We have seen the service-delivery protests. It is unacceptable that twenty years after independence, there are still some communities that use the bucket system, that not everyone has running water in their homes, that schools don't have textbooks and children still have to cross rivers to go to school. Something must be done. We need to build a world in which our children and their children can live peacefully.

In closing, I would like to emphasise the values of accountability and responsibility. We are accountable to the Creator for our lives and we are responsible to Him for how our lives work out. So life is a continuous process of change and choice – choice about how you conduct yourself and who you associate with. Someone once said, "If you run with the wolves, you will learn how to howl, but if you associate with eagles, you will learn how to soar."

MaAfrika, let us soar like eagles to greater and greater heights.

# AUTHOR'S NOTE

My husband Sol and I nurtured our family over sixty years. We raised six children, who subsequently had their own households and children. In raising our children, we established certain family traditions including regular meetings, giving each family member household tasks and a sustained focus on family education.

We also formed a constitution to ensure that what we had created would be continued and improved upon by future generations. My family – the Sol-Con family – has grown larger and more complex. Over the next sixty years, it will become difficult to recognise some relatives as the family will have grown beyond recognition. It was our hope that having a constitution would create a platform for family members to meet up and connect, a system to ensure that all family members are welcomed and recognised within the family.

I believe many families could benefit from having a constitution. A constitution helps unite relatives by being explicit about the family's mission and values. It is important that such a constitution remains a living document, that everyone feels as though they have a say in its terms and that it adapts to meet the needs of a changing world. Its goal is to ensure that individual members and the family collective work together to address broader family activities. It is a compass for the future.

# THE NGCABA FAMILY CONSTITUTION

### Vision
The Sol-Con family, as a caring family, will strive for unity of its members and their ability to feed themselves in a self-sufficient manner.

### Mission
The vision will be achieved by educating family members and encouraging members to work hard during their lives.

### Organisational structures
The family will have an assembly, a council and a family office. The chairperson of the assembly will be elected every year, as will the secretary, treasurer and organising committee members.

### Committees
The family will form the following committees, among others:

• *The Younger Generation Committee* will develop a charter for members of the younger generation to address issues relating to this age cohort. This committee will also be responsible for drafting the family's Code of Ethics.

• *The Family Relations Committee* will ensure that family relations are always cordial.

• *The Conflict Resolution Committee* will listen to and resolve any conflict arising between family members.

• *The Family Support Committee* will manage requests for help, whether financial or practical, from members of the family who need support due to circumstances beyond their control.

• *The Geriatrics and Family Support committees* will manage a family care programme for elderly members of the family and those who are in need of care.

• *The Sol-Con Brand Committee* will develop and manage the Sol-Con brand going forward. All family members wanting to use the brand will have to subscribe to the Sol-Con brand values.

Establishing committees is very important. These committees are required to meet at least once a year to deliberate and structure their activities. Members should write to the committee chairperson to raise issues. Electronic engagement is encouraged.

## Individual family members

All family members will have rights and responsibilities to the family, as detailed later. Family members are also expected to develop a personal development programme for their own personal growth.

## Finances

The following funds will be created:

- A *voluntary mutual fund* will be established to benefit those who participate directly in the fund. This will be governed like any investment structure.
- A *voluntary family education fund* will be established to help those members of the family who cannot afford an education. The fund will act as a guarantee for a bank loan. The beneficiary will have to repay the loan upon entering the workforce.
- A *voluntary futures investment fund* will be created to help the family with governance and constitutional matters. This includes educating the next generation about the constitution and its respective structures.
- A *family history fund* will be created to help fund continued research into the family's history and the ongoing documentation of family events.

This will help to encourage future generations to excel and be good citizens.

## Responsibilities of individual members

Family members are required to:

- Work to support themselves, their children and their parents. This ethic of work should extend to all family members, including children.
- Complete assigned or chosen tasks for the good of the family or society as a whole.
- Conduct their individual and collective activities in a trustworthy manner. Trust is the basis for working together as a family.
- Strive for unity of the collective and their respective family units.
- Care for family members who are less fortunate. The happiness of the individual is linked to the happiness of the family. This happiness should be something that all members work towards achieving, with the understanding that happiness means different things to different people.
- Develop a personal happiness charter.

- Ensure that their wills, estate plans and letters of wishes are in order to provide certainty when they are gone. This will avoid family feuds.
- Buy life policies, insurance and other products to ensure that their death does not incur more pain than is necessary for those they leave behind.

Family members are encouraged to:
- Acquire a medical-aid policy.
- Undergo psychometric or psychological analysis on a regular basis to establish gene-related issues. The family will establish a relationship with a psychometric analyst and a psychologist for this purpose.
- Record and store their genetic code (in accordance with the laws of the country).
- Establish relations with philanthropic structures and civil structures, both in their individual capacity and as a member of the Ngcaba family.
- Expand their interests beyond the borders of South Africa and become global citizens. This can be done through their professional careers or business opportunities.

**Household responsibilities**
Each family unit is expected to:
- Develop work plans for children between the ages of six and twenty-two. This work plan can start with simple household chores like doing the dishes or making the bed and progress to working during the school holidays as the child gets older. This will help foster a good work ethic, which is central to the family's values.
- Have a local family doctor.
- Frequently and openly express love, especially parental love. Familial love is what bonds the family together. It should be nurtured at all times.

**General resolutions**
*Communications*
An online family portal will be created and used to communicate important announcements and events to the collective.
*Family database*
There is no future without a past. A deep understanding of the family's background and geography should be part of common family knowledge. A family tree with clan names, ancestral names and positions will be created and made available to all generations.
*Additions to the family*
All children born to the Ngcaba family will be automatically included in the family structure and will have the same rights and benefits as existing members. This includes children born to surrogates and adopted children, provided these activities

are done in terms of the laws of the country. People marrying into the family will be inducted into the family no later than three months after joining.

*Tombstone unveiling*

Tombstone unveiling events should take place five to ten years after a family member's death. Yearly graveyard visits and cleaning is encouraged.

*Death*

A protocol for managing death and related events should be developed and signed by all adults in the family. Dealing with death can seriously affect a person's mental health, especially in the elderly. The family should take steps to help grieving family members if needed.

*Family education*

- Family education is one of the Sol-Con family values. It extends beyond formal schooling to include ongoing education on a range of topics, including financial management and self-development.
- A family education programme should be put in place to ensure the ongoing education of family members of all generations. This programme should be customised to each generation's needs. Senior family members should ensure that all junior members' educational needs are provided for.
- A family certification process should be developed to recognise those who have gone through certain phases of family education. Learning sessions should be recorded to credit members for attendance.

*Religion and spirituality*

The Sol-Con family value system emanates from Christianity. Family members are encouraged to register with the Methodist church in their neighbourhood and children are urged to attend Sunday school every week.

*Family culture and traditions*

- Culture is an embodiment of who we are. Cultural norms are not static; they should evolve to meet the needs of younger generations.
- The Sol-Con family's traditional code is based on Christian values, coupled with a scientific approach. It is also based on our ancestral framework. The code will be written down to act as a guide for new members entering the family. This guide will cover issues such as language and the traditions followed at certain landmarks in life (for example, birth, death and marriage).

*Amendments*

The constitution may be amended every twenty years.

Printed in the United States
By Bookmasters